ere are a few of the Pack Ventures carried out by Brownies in different parts of the country

17th CHELTENHAM (BETHESDA), GLOUCESTERSHIRE

1. Orga[illegible] swim to raise funds

2. Ente[illegible] with uniforms o[illegible]

6th PE[illegible]LINGTON

3. Ente[illegible], made by themse[illegible]

4. Des[illegible]fee morning, fo[illegible]

1
2
3
4

1st DANBURY, ESSEX

5. With another Pack made a film of a Brownie meeting to send to Brownie Scouts in America

1st WILFORD, NOTTINGHAMSHIRE

6. Spent four evenings polishing the pews of the village church

5
6

12/-
60 p

For BROWNIE GUIDES Everywhere

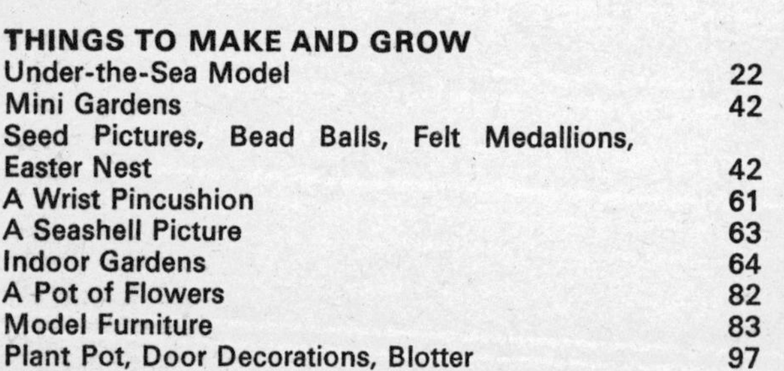

Made and printed in Great Britain by PURNELL & SONS LTD., Paulton (Somerset) and London

THE BROWNIE ANNUAL

for 1971

Published by special arrangement with THE GIRL GUIDES ASSOCIATION

Illustrated by PHIL GASCOINE

PURNELL
London, W.1

SBN 361 01495 3

The Brownie who *Dared*

by Barbara Beacham

Julie threw the beret angrily across the room

Great-Aunt Elizabeth twitched the parlour curtain into place and "tut-tutted" under her breath. Really, it was too bad of George and Susan to go off to New Zealand like that and leave their nine-year-old daughter behind so that someone else had to look after her. Julie was altogether too much of a handful, far too high-spirited, and not at all ladylike in behaviour. Just look at her now, skipping along with one foot on the pavement and one in the gutter! As for that absurd brown uniform she was wearing, going to meetings and calling herself a Brown Guide or some such foolish name—well, it was all beyond her, and Great-Aunt Elizabeth "tut-tutted" again and went to the front door in answer to Julie's impatient ring.

"Oh, Aunt Elizabeth," cried Julie, the moment the door was opened, "we had such fun at Brownies tonight, and Brown Owl is every bit as nice as my Brown Owl at home. Pauline—she's my new Sixer—and Fiona are ever so nice, and after the holidays they said I must go to tea with them, and do you know they were asking me all sorts of questions about my Pack at home, and what do you think——?"

"I think," said Great-Aunt Elizabeth in a cold, flat voice, "that you are talking far too much and too loudly. Really, it is of very little interest to me to know what went on this evening. In my youth children were seen and not heard, and were never allowed to talk as you do."

Julie looked like a pricked balloon. The eager expression died out of her face, and her mouth drooped. Why was Great-Aunt Elizabeth so horrid? She never seemed to be interested in anything—not like Mother, who wanted to know everything. If only Mother were here! She would love to know about the meeting, what sort of questions the Brownies had asked, and what Brown Owl was like. But Great-Aunt Elizabeth was not in the slightest degree interested.

"I'm sorry." Julie mumbled now. "I think I'll go to bed. Goodnight, Aunt Elizabeth!"

"Goodnight, Julie." Great-Aunt Elizabeth bent stiffly and gave her great-niece a peck on the forehead.

Once in her room Julie gave vent to her feelings by throwing her Brownie beret across the room. It landed on a pretty china ornament in the shape of a kitten on the mantelpiece. Julie saw the ornament begin to fall and darted forward, but she

It landed on the ornament, which toppled over

was too late and the china kitten lay in pieces in the hearth.

Julie was appalled. For a moment she stood staring at the pieces, then she went down on her hands and knees and began to gather them up. She turned over her Brownie beret and put the pieces carefully inside. Perhaps the kitten could be glued together again!

Slow tears welled in Julie's eyes. Oh, if only Mother were here! She would know that she hadn't meant to break the dear little china kitten. It was the only pretty thing in her unlovely room. Whatever would Great-Aunt Elizabeth say? *She* would never understand that Julie loved the china kitten and that breaking it was an accident.

"What are you hiding in your hat, Julie?" demanded Great-Aunt Elizabeth from the doorway.

Julie jumped guiltily and tried to answer, but she couldn't find her voice. She hadn't heard her aunt at the door. She stayed on the floor, staring at her aunt, big brown eyes full of tears.

Great-Aunt Elizabeth rustled across the room and took Julie's beret from her. "My china kitten!" she cried. "You wicked girl! You have broken my kitten ornament, and you were obviously going to hide the pieces without telling me. I suppose, too, you were going to let the blame fall on Mrs. Norton."

At this Julie found her voice. "I wasn't, I wasn't! You don't understand. I didn't mean to break it. I loved it, and of course I'd have told you."

"Why, then, were you hiding the pieces in your hat?" demanded Great-Aunt Elizabeth icily. "I am shocked, Julie. You are untruthful."

"I'm not," cried Julie, scrambling to her feet. "I don't tell lies. I wasn't hiding the pieces. I was picking them up."

"Why did you not use the wastepaper basket?"

"Because my beret is soft and wouldn't damage the pieces." Julie knew her answer must sound absurd to Great-Aunt Elizabeth, who wouldn't think the china kitten could be mended.

"Damage pieces of broken china!" The scorn in Great-Aunt Elizabeth's voice made Julie cower back. "I never heard anything so ridiculous in my life." Great-Aunt Elizabeth shook the beret and made the china pieces rattle inside. Then she eyed Julie sternly. "As they do not teach you to tell the truth at Brownies, you will go no more."

"Go no more!" Julie repeated. "Oh, but they do teach us to tell the truth, and I don't tell lies!"

Great-Aunt Elizabeth shook the beret again. The china kitten's head fell out and landed on her shoe. She picked it up and looked at it, her lips pursed.

"I am very cross about this, Julie," she said.

When she finally stalked out of the room, she left Julie white-faced and miserable. She was to have no pocket money for weeks and weeks—not until there was enough money to buy another china kitten. Even worse, she was not to go to Brownies again.

As the days went by, Julie's resentment against Great-Aunt Elizabeth grew. School broke up for the holidays. Pauline and Fiona went away. Julie was lonely and unhappy. Things improved a little when she went back to school again, but then came the first Pack meeting since she broke the ornament.

Julie looked at her aunt across the tea-table. Her aunt was sitting behind the silver tea-tray, her spectacles on the end of her nose, pouring herself a cup of tea. Julie wondered for the hundredth time how she could have become related to someone like Great-Aunt Elizabeth.

"It's Brownies tonight," she said. "Please can I go, Aunt Elizabeth?"

Great-Aunt Elizabeth put down the teapot. "I have told you, Julie, that while you are in my charge there will be no more Brownie meetings for you."

"But, Aunt Elizabeth," cried Julie, "you're not being fair. I didn't mean to break the ornament, and I'm sorry. Please let me go to Brownies."

"No!" Great-Aunt Elizabeth adjusted her spectacles and looked at Julie. "When I say no, I mean no."

"It's not fair!" Suddenly Julie exploded. "You're horrid. You won't let me do anything. I hate you!"

Jumping to her feet, she ran out of the room and up the stairs to her bedroom,

"I shall lock you in," Great-Aunt Elizabeth said coldly

where she flung herself on her bed and burst into tears.

Great-Aunt Elizabeth followed her and stood in the doorway. "I can see you are in a mood to defy me," she said coldly, "and as I do not intend that you should go to Brownies, I shall lock you in."

"Lock me in!" cried Julie aghast. "Oh, no!"

But her aunt shut the door and turned the key in the lock.

Julie sat on the bed staring at the door. She was locked in like a naughty little girl! It wasn't fair! Why was Great-Aunt Elizabeth so unkind? Well, she jolly well would go to Brownies!

She jumped from the bed and put on her Brownie uniform. When she was dressed she hurried to the door. It had not sounded as if the key had been taken out of the lock. If it hadn't been it might be possible to poke it out and pull it back under the door. She stooped down and put her eye to the keyhole. Then she saw the landing wallpaper. The key had gone!

Julie stamped her foot and rattled the door-handle. Then she gave a little sob and leant against the door. Catching sight of herself in the dressing-table mirror, she saw such a miserable face staring back at her that she began to realise that she was not behaving much like a Brownie. She felt wretched, but there was no need to go on hating someone, however horrid. As she began to think about her aunt, she heard her shut the bedroom door across the landing and go downstairs. Then came a sudden shrill scream, followed by a series of thuds.

Julie stared back at her shocked face in the mirror. The meaning of the noises became clear in her mind. Great-Aunt Elizabeth must have fallen down the stairs.

Suddenly Julie remembered something her mother had said to her: "Great-Aunt Elizabeth is old and very lonely, Julie, and has never had anyone to love her."

"Lock me in!" cried Julie, aghast. "Oh, no!"

Julie rushed to the door and rattled it loudly. "Aunt Elizabeth, what's happened? What have you done? Please let me out."

There was no reply to her calls. She rattled the handle again, and called again, but no answer came.

"Mrs. Norton's gone," she told herself, "and I can't get out. Oh, whatever shall I do?"

She ran to the window. Her bedroom looked out on to the back garden. There was a long, straight drop to the path. Could she, dare she, jump? She drew back, knowing that she could not. If only she had a rope she could let herself down, but there was no rope in the bedroom. Then she saw the tree.

The tree grew in the middle of the back garden, but its branches spread out to quite near the house. There was one branch that came within reach of her window—just! If she were brave enough, she might be able to climb out of the window and swing across to the main trunk by way of the branch.

She drew a deep breath. It was terribly risky. She might easily fall, and the distance to the ground was quite frightening. But she could not leave her aunt downstairs and not make some effort to get help to her. Great-Aunt Elizabeth might be lying unconscious there.

Pushing up the window, Julie climbed carefully out. She dared not look down, but kept her eyes fixed steadily on the branch that reached out towards her. It had seemed close to the house when she first glanced at it, but when her safety depended upon her grasping it the distance from the window seemed like that of a great, yawning gulf.

"I've got to do it!" Julie whispered. Letting her legs dangle from the sill,

Julie launched herself out and grabbed the branch

she screwed up her courage, reached out both hands towards the thick branch and gave a spring forward. She shut her eyes as she launched herself out. For one terrifying moment she thought she had clutched at empty space, but next instant her hands felt rough bark under them, and she grasped fiercely at the branch, and held on.

For a second or two she hung suspended by her hands and arms above the ground; then she hauled herself up on to the branch and rested there, gasping. The worst was over, but she still had to climb along the branch to the main trunk and then get down to the ground.

Cautiously, inch by inch, trying hard not to look down at the ground so far below her, she wriggled along the branch until she was able to gain a firm foothold on a lower branch, from whence it was comparatively easy to reach the trunk and lower herself, step by step, to the ground.

She was scratched and bleeding from where twigs and branches had caught her skin, and her uniform was torn, but she paid no attention to any damage done. She had to find out what had happened to Great-Aunt Elizabeth and, if need be, go for help.

Just as she straightened up, she saw Mrs. Norton, her aunt's daily help, passing along the pavement that ran alongside the front of the house, and she called out urgently.

"Mrs. Norton, please—I think my aunt's had a fall. Could you come in with me and see if she's all right?"

"Goodness me!" cried Mrs. Norton. "Whatever's happened? What a state you're in, dearie! Your aunt, you say? Yes, yes, I'll come in with you, of course!"

As the front door was locked, Julie had to climb in through a window to let Mrs. Norton in. Great-Aunt Elizabeth was lying in a heap at the foot of the stairs. As Julie bent over her, she opened her eyes.

"Is that you, Julie—oh, and you, Mrs. Norton! What has happened?"

"I think you must have fallen down the

stairs, Aunt Elizabeth," Julie told her.

"We'll get you into a chair," said Mrs. Norton briskly. "Can you lend a hand, Julie?"

Julie nodded. Between them they managed to get Aunt Elizabeth into an armchair and make her comfortable. She had received a shock rather than physical damage, and under the ministrations of Julie and Mrs. Norton she soon began to recover.

"I don't know how long I should have stayed there if you hadn't come to the rescue," she said, as she accepted a cup of tea from Mrs. Norton. "How did you get in?"

Mrs. Norton jerked a thumb at Julie. "You've got to thank your plucky little niece for it all," she told Aunt Elizabeth. "She climbed out of her bedroom window to reach the tree so that she could bring help to you. A nice old mess she's in too!"

"Julie climbed out——!" Aunt Elizabeth gazed at Julie, startled. "Oh, I remember now! I locked you in. Oh, dear, dear me! Tell me about it, Julie," she said abruptly.

Julie told her what had happened. "I'm sorry, Aunt Elizabeth," she ended. "I couldn't open the door, and I was horribly afraid that you were lying there helpless. I just had to get out to fetch help!"

"You did a very brave and wonderful thing," said her aunt slowly, "and I'm very ashamed of my treatment of you, Julie. I can only say thank you for what you did and ask you to forgive me for my unkindness to you."

Impulsively, Julie flung her arms round her aunt's neck. "Oh, I don't want thanking. I only want you to be happy, Aunt Elizabeth—like me!"

"I think we're going to be happy together from now on," said her aunt quietly, "very happy indeed!"

"Hope these Brownies will come again," mumbles Charlie through a beakful of Brownie cake supplied by (left to right) Cindy, Elizabeth, Clare and Patricia

BROWNIES IN BIRDLAND

by
THE EDITOR

Photos by Harry Hammond

"Goodbye!" cried the cockatoo as soon as we set foot in Birdland.

We thought this was a rather odd kind of welcome—to be bidden good-bye just as we arrived! But there are quite a few oddities in Birdland—like Charlie, the blue-and-gold macaw who likes to hang upside-down from a tree and shout "Hello!" and "Oi!" to visitors; or the African grey parrot, Juno, who loves to show off by doing acrobatics. Juno is one of the favourite birds of Mr. Leonard Hill, the friendly owner of Birdland. When Mr. Hill calls out "Bedtime!" from the window of his house, Juno flies in to bed from wherever he may be.

Four Brownies from the 17th Cheltenham (Bethesda) Pack came with me to Birdland. They are Cindy Smithers, Elizabeth Pixley, Clare Blomfield, and Patricia Charles. You can see them with the birds in the photographs, and you can see Cindy and Elizabeth with George, a scarlet-and-gold macaw, in the lovely picture in colour on the front of this annual.

George the macaw takes a fancy to Cindy

Can you see a bird in Cindy's hand in the cover picture? It is Juno, lying on his back ready to be spun round like a top. He lay quite still while the photograph was taken, but he had to be spun round afterwards!

There are six hundred birds at Birdland, some of them birds that might have become extinct if they hadn't been preserved and looked after in a place where they could breed again. Mr. Hill has loved birds since he was a boy, and he went with Mr. Peter Scott to the Antarctic for the penguins that you can see diving for fish in a big glass tank at Birdland. Some of the birds are almost unbelievable. One of these is the hornbill, which lived 5,000 feet up in the Himalayas and carries a beak or bill so enormous that it must be a burden to him. Another is the bower bird, who looks quite aristocratic and who is a wonderful mimic. One of the most remarkable mimics is the mynah bird, who makes you look round indignantly when you hear someone near you say "Hello, cocky!" or "Heh, you!" His "voice" sounds so human that you can hardly believe it is a bird "speaking."

I specially enjoyed one beautifully coloured bird of the partridge family who followed me round when I crumbled up a soft sweet. It pecked up the sweet crumbs from my hand and enabled other visitors to get close-up snapshots of it.

"Aren't they comical?" Cindy and Elizabeth tell each other about the antics of the birds they have seen. "I trust they're not referring to me as comical," says the flamingo, with dignity

"Just watch us," the penguin advises the Brownies. "We're the star performers of Birdland"

Among a variety of ducks is Donald, who is very tame and will follow visitors round like a dog. Patrick the Pelican is the mascot of airmen at an R.A.F. station near. On special occasions he is "dressed up" in a bow-tie.

We tried to take photographs of the Brownies feeding the flamingoes, but flamingoes are very timid and hurried away on their long, slender legs as soon as the Brownies drew near.

There is a lot of fun and entertainment to be gained by a visit to Birdland, but don't forget that it is a bird sanctuary and that the birds in it are very valuable, and some of them rare. A film was made of Birdland, which is known all over the world and visited by many distinguished people. Birdland is in the very pretty Cotswold village of Bourton-on-the-Water, which is not far from Cheltenham (Gloucestershire) and Chipping Norton (Oxfordshire). If your Pack is in a town within reach of it, you will find it a quite rewarding place for a Pack outing. Mr. Hill, who created it, likes children and goes to endless trouble to make their visit interesting and enjoyable as well as instructive. Our Brownies, of course, didn't forget to say a big thank-you to him when they left.

—R.M.

"Go on – tell me the time, as you think you're so clever," challenges George, flying up on to the sundial by Clare and Patricia

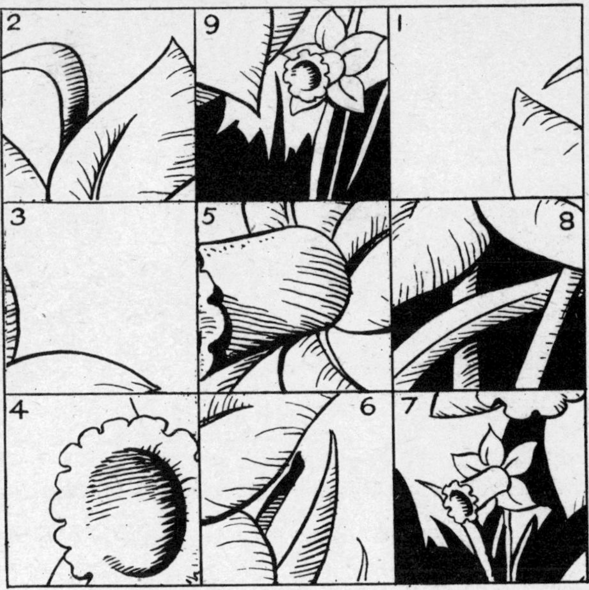

WHICH GUIDE PATROL WILL YOU GO IN?

When you go up to Guides you may be in a Patrol named after a bird, a flower or a tree. This picture jigsaw puzzle represents a Guide Patrol. To find out what it is, copy the drawing in each frame above into the frame below with the same number. Then you will see the whole picture and know the name of the Guide Patrol.

"Look, I'm slipping in!" is what Patricia seems to be saying. Well, she'll only get her feet wet, for Bourton-on-the-Water's pretty river is only shallow

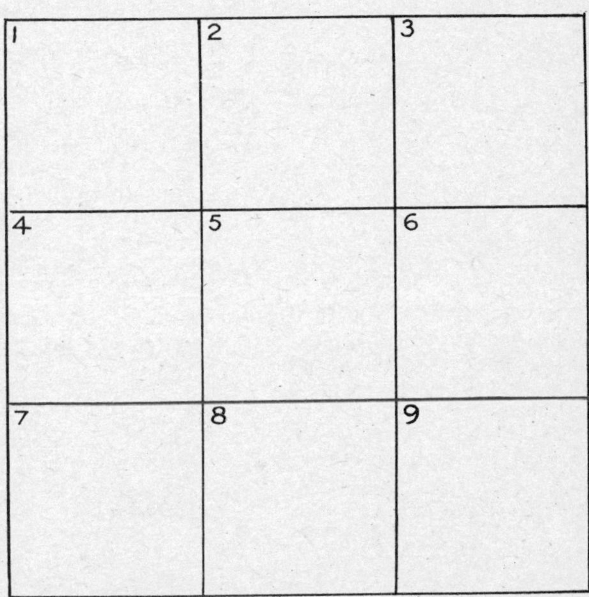

WHO?

by

Jean Kenward

Who saw the cherry
That hung on the bough?
"I", said the blackbird;
"It's mine now!"

Who saw the apple
That fell on the grass?
"I", said the ant;
"I could not pass."

Who saw the grape
On its curling vine?
"I", said the wasp;
"At dinner time!"

Who saw the peach
That flushed on the wall?
"I", said the girl;
"I ate it all!"

NATURE QUIZ

Can you pair up these nuts and berries with their leaves?

Answers

A – 4 Wild Rose
B – 2 Sycamore
C – 5 Pine
D – 3 Oak
E – 6 Blackberry
F – 1 Horsechestnut

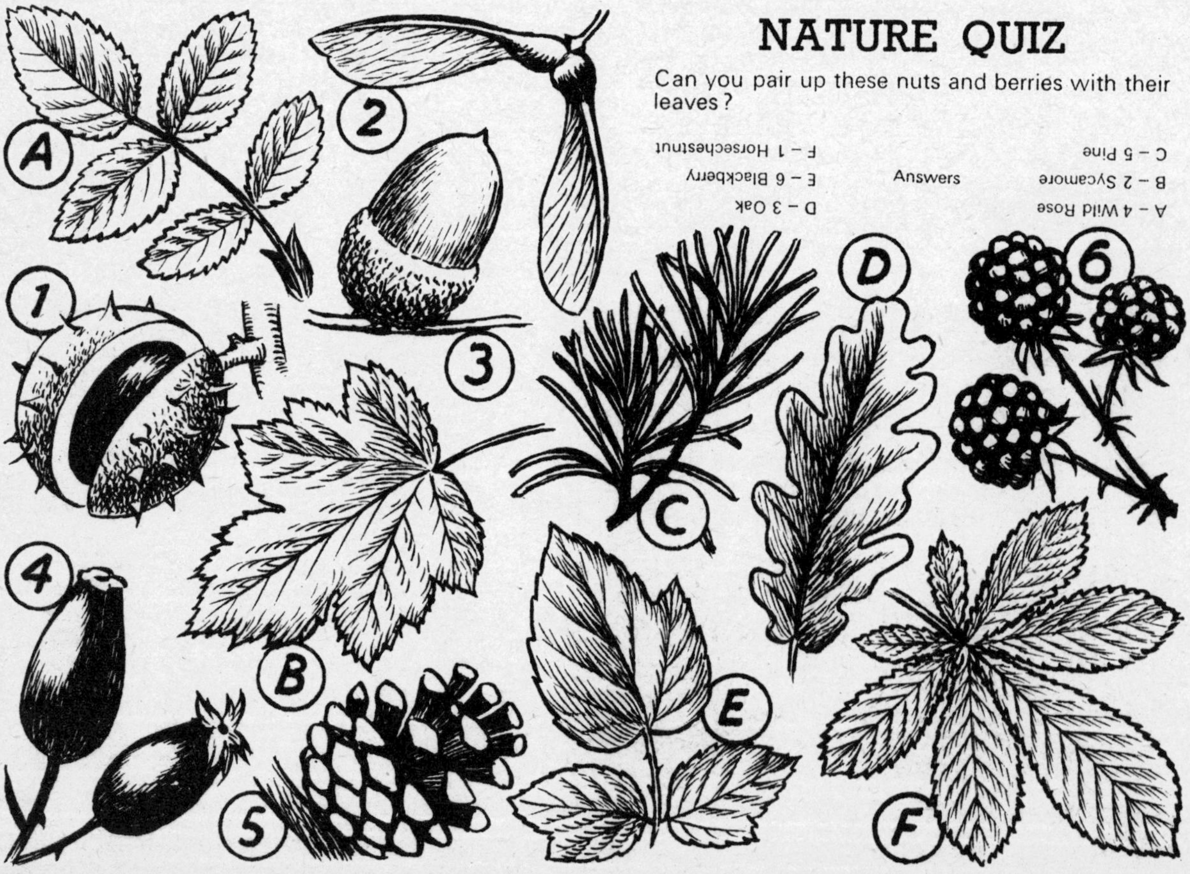

APRIL FOOL

by

Aileen E. Passmore

If anyone says, Go and look at the bear
 In the orchard with eyes round and red,
Or the man in the chimney with long purple hair,
 Or the scarecrow upstairs in your bed,

It's best to risk being a Fool and go,
For though it's unlikely—you never know!

THE WISE OWL SAYS

Those who bring sunshine into the lives of others cannot keep it from themselves.

A Bible in hand is worth two on the shelf.

The trouble with letting off steam is that you only get into more hot water.

To be a success in anything, as in music, you must practise the hard parts.

Don't let your parents down—they brought you up.

Don't live your life as if you were in a cafeteria, where there is self-service only.

Of all things you wear, your expression is the most important.

Reading is to the mind what exercise is to the body.

The faults of others are like the headlamps of a car—they only seem more glaring than your own.

Learn to enjoy the simple things of life. They cost least; they last longest.

Seven prayerless days make one weak.

Rudeness is the weak girl's imitation of strength.

Being shy may mean that you are thinking more about your own feelings than about other people's.

Many a false step is made by standing still.

If you know what hurts you you know what hurts others.

Life is like a game of tennis. The one who serves best wins most.

Speed gets you nowhere if you're going in the wrong direction.

Hazel's First Challenge

by
Christine Hornsby

Hazel sat on the window-seat in her new home. Her legs were drawn up to her chin. Outside the rain fell steadily, but Hazel could not hear the sound that the raindrops made against the window-pane, for she was almost totally deaf. Hers was a silent world and often a lonely one, for the other children in the neighbourhood knew that she was different and never seemed to want to play with her. Her mother, feeling for her in her loneliness, moved across the room and put a hand upon her shoulder.

At her touch, Hazel turned and smiled. "Yes, Mummy? Did you want something?" she asked.

"We've been in our new home for over a month now, dear, and you haven't made any friends; so I have arranged for you to join the Brownies. A friend of mine is calling for you this evening. Her own daughter is a Brownie, and she says it is great fun."

Hazel's eyes lit up as she lip-read her mother's words. The thought of a new playmate made her feel much, much better, and at once she rushed upstairs to wash and change out of her jeans. Later that afternoon she found herself sitting in a car opposite Caroline, who told her about the 1st Hamilton Brownie Guide Pack, Hazel reading the words from the way Caroline formed them with her lips.

Brownies turned out to be every bit as much fun as Caroline had said it would be, and Brown Owl and Tawny Owl were most kind and thoughtful about Hazel's difficulty in hearing. Hazel's problems were still there, though, for she always was the last to do everything and often failed to understand at once what was expected of her. The Brownies themselves tried to

As she tied her shoelace, Hazel read the youth's lips

be helpful, and especially Caroline, but they often forgot to speak directly to her, which was the only way Hazel could understand what they were saying.

At the meeting at which Hazel made her Promise, Brownies of the Pack received their first Venture badge for a Pack Venture, in which all had taken part. Hazel wondered wistfully whether she would be able to join in the next Venture—or in later ones, either! Unless she could lip-read all that was said about it she might not know what had to be done, and she wouldn't like to keep asking Brown Owl or Tawny.

As she made her way home that evening, she worried about it. She loved Brownies and badly wanted to be a useful member of the Sprites and of the Pack, but if she couldn't hear——

Her thoughts broke off. Ahead of her two youths were standing with their bikes outside a cottage that Hazel knew belonged to an old lady everybody called Granny Robinson. Hazel hesitated when she saw them because they looked rather rough types. She was wondering whether to turn back or go on as boldly as she could when her face suddenly paled. The youths were facing her and talking earnestly to each other. As a matter of habit, though without any particular curiosity about what they were saying, Hazel read their moving lips, and suddenly and swiftly bent to tie her shoelace. What the two youths were saying appalled her.

"You needn't worry, Joe. There ain't no risk. Granny Robinson gets off the seven o'clock bus. I've watched regularly, so I know. We'll give 'er 'alf an hour to get 'ere, and then do our stuff."

"It sounds a pushover," admitted the other. "It'd be worth the risk for a month's cash, but it ain't worth doing if she's only got a bit on 'er."

"There'll be plenty, an' we'll be away on our bikes before she 'as a chance to recognise us. It's easy money."

Hazel straightened up. She needed all her courage to walk on past the two youths, but she didn't dare turn and run, as she badly wanted to do. If she did, their suspicions might be aroused. As it was, they couldn't possibly suspect that she had heard what they said; she was too far away.

Her heart beat fast as she hurried past the youths, who eyed her narrowly but did not make any attempt to molest her.

As soon as she was out of their view, she took to her heels and ran. The lane was deserted, and her own house was quite a long distance away. She wasn't sure of the time. The youths had specified seven o'clock as the time at which Granny Robinson got off the bus. Not having been long in the village of Little Hamilton, Hazel didn't know where the bus stopped. It might well be that Granny Robinson would get off it at the other end of the lane and that the youths would waylay her before she reached her cottage. They were certainly after her money.

Hazel ran until she felt her heart would burst and her legs collapse under her. Then she saw a car draw up at the kerb beside her and saw Brown Owl's head appear through a window.

"Why, it's you, Hazel! Hello, is anything the matter? You seem quite distressed."

Concerned, Brown Owl jumped out of the car. Jerkily, Hazel told her what she had discovered by reading the lips of the two youths.

"Good heavens! Poor Granny Robinson! It sounds very much as if they are planning to rob her of her pension, which I believe she draws from the post-office at Grimstow once a month when she goes to visit her sister. We must act quickly. It's gone seven now. There isn't a moment to lose. You can help, Hazel. Will you run down to the police-station and tell Constable Briggs what you have told me? I will drive back at once to the bus stop where Granny Robinson is likely to get off for her cottage. I may be in time to prevent her from being robbed or coming to harm."

Hazel nodded and sped away. Brown Owl hurried back into her car, turned it, and drove swiftly back the way she had come.

Constable Briggs, in charge of the single police-station at Little Hamilton, rubbed his hands on hearing Hazel's story.

Constable Briggs ended their struggles by banging their heads together

"I'll get them louts, never fear, missy," he declared. "They've been seen around the village quite a bit lately, and caused bothers. Now, you go straight on home and leave everything to me."

But Hazel didn't go straight on home. She was so eager to see the outcome of it all that when Constable Briggs mounted his bicycle and rode off as fast as his great bulk would allow in the direction of Granny Robinson's cottage, she followed. By doing this, she was just in time to see the climax of the whole drama.

Constable Briggs dismounted outside Granny Robinson's cottage, leaned his bike against the garden wall, and started up the path to the cottage. As he opened the gate, two youths who were hiding in the bushes and rank grass beside the path of the overgrown garden jumped up in panic and charged for the gate. But Constable Briggs was so large that he almost filled the path. He was immensely strong, and he grabbed a youth with each hand as they ran and held them. They both struggled violently and lashed out at him with their fists and then with their feet, whereupon Constable Briggs banged their heads together, none too gently, and took all the fight out of them.

A few minutes later, Brown Owl's car stopped outside the cottage, and Granny Robinson stepped out.

"I was just in time to pick Granny up at the bus stop," explained Brown Owl. "I've told her that we feared these youths intended to rob her, and she is very grateful, especially to Hazel here. I see you've got them safely, Constable Briggs."

"They won't get away from me, ma'am, never fear," the constable assured her, "and I've got a charge against 'em that'll stand up in court too. I'll take 'em down to the station, ma'am, and I'll take a statement from you and the little missy later."

"I'll see Granny safely into her cottage," said Brown Owl, "and then I'll take Hazel home and explain to her mother why she's so late."

"I told her to go straight on home," said the constable, smiling, "but I reckon I shan't be complaining one little bit about her not doing as I told her! She's a plucky 'un, she is."

So Hazel's adventure ended very satisfactorily for all except the two youths, who were put on probation and were never seen in the district again. It had one unexpected and quite delightful sequel too. At the next Pack meeting, Brown Owl told the Brownies of the brave and clever way in which Hazel had acted to save old Granny Robinson from being hurt and robbed. The Pack, of course, were greatly impressed by this.

In Pow-wow they were invited to put forward ideas for a new Pack Venture. Rather timidly Hazel said, "Please, Brown Owl, I noticed that Granny Robinson's garden was badly overgrown and very untidy. I expect she's too weak to look after it. Could the Pack make it look nice for her, do you think?"

Brown Owl, Tawny and the whole Pack voted this a first-class idea for a Venture.

So, despite her deafness, Hazel proved herself to be a very useful member of the Pack, able to suggest a helpful and interesting Pack Venture, and join happily in carrying it out.

MAKE THIS UNDER-THE-SEA MODEL

M. I. Eckhardt Shows You How

Materials required are 1 cardboard box, 1 sheet of stiff card, green cotton, paints, scissors, coloured chocolate wrappers or other shiny paper, shells, glue.

Paint the back of the cardboard box green-blue. Paint seaweed on it when dry. Paint the bottom of the box sandy-brown. Stick real shells on the bottom when dry. Paint the sides of the box greeny-blue.

Draw fish shapes and cut out. Cover them with your shiny paper. Make a small hole in the middle of the fishes' backs and thread green cotton through. Make several holes in the top of your cardboard box; then you can push your cotton up through these holes and knot it at the top. It is better to use different lengths of cotton.

Draw crab shapes and paint. Cut out also a thin piece of card to act as a prop. This will enable the crabs to stand on the sea bed.

Finally, cover the front of the box with transparent paper so that you and your friends can see under the sea.

Try These Riddles on Your Friends

When is water not water?
When it is dripping.

Which burns longer, a wax candle or a tallow candle?
Neither—they both burn shorter.

What matches aren't kept in a box?
Cricket matches.

What sleeper never wakes up?
A railway sleeper.

Why is Ireland like a large shop where butter is sold?
Because it is full of little Pats.

What drum can never be beaten?
Your ear-drum.

What blade never needs sharpening?
Your shoulder blade.

What cups don't need saucers?
Buttercups.

A very heavy fall of snow has blocked many roads in the country town. How will the Brownies get to Pack meeting? See if you can find the right way to the Pack meeting hall. You can't pass any barriers to get there.

CLUES
1. It's silvery and graceful
2. It sounds as if it grows by the sea, but it doesn't
3. It's prickly, an evergreen, and popular at Christmas
4. May blossom grows on it
5. It's a tree with "keys" on it
6. Another name for this is the lind

KNOW YOUR TREES

These Pictures Will Help You Find Them

Can you name the trees in the wood from these pictures of them or from the leaves? That's what the two Brownies, Karen and Jill, are trying to do. They're working for the Discoverer badge. If you name the trees first this will help you to solve the puzzle, but you can do it the other way round if you like—solve the clues and write in the names of the trees in the leaf; then find the trees in the wood.

by
M. J. ECKHARDT

has "wings" on it

ANSWERS: 1-Birch; 2-Beech; 3-Holly; 4-Hawthorn; 5-Ash; 6-Lime; 7-Sycamore.

The Patrol That Changed Its Name

An Exciting Guide Adventure in Pictures by Robert Moss

BECAME INVOLVED IN A HEATED DISCUSSION STARTED BY STORM ....

WHY CAN'T WE BE **DIFFERENT?** WHY CAN'T WE TAKE THE NAME OF AN UNCOMMON BIRD, INSTEAD OF THE OWL?

BECAUSE, STORMY, AS B.-P. ADVISED, IT WOULD BE SILLY TO CALL OURSELVES SOMETHING LIKE THE ALBATROSS PATROL WHEN WE HAVEN'T THE FAINTEST CHANCE OF STUDYING THE ALBATROSS!

SO STORM'S IDEA WAS TURNED DOWN, AND NO MORE WAS HEARD OF IT DURING THE BUSY DAYS OF PREPARING FOR THE COMPANY'S CAMP, SITED IN A WILD AND MOUNTAINOUS PART OF NORTHUMBERLAND.......

THEY STUMBLED ON THROUGH THE THICK BLANKET OF MIST TILL STORM HAD TO STOP AND RETIE A SHOELACE. ANNE TOOK THE LEAD.....

SUDDENLY THE MIST ROLLED AWAY, REVEALING DEADLY PERIL

A SURPRISE AWAITED THE GUIDES ....

STORM AND ANNE RETRACED THEIR STEPS UNTIL AT LAST THEY WERE HAILED BY LAURA, AT THE HEAD OF A SEARCH-PARTY ......

EARLY NEXT MORNING....
I'M DETECTIVE-SERGEANT CONNELL. MR. GAVIN TOLD ME WHAT YOU GUIDES SAW ON THE MOUNTAIN. I'D LIKE YOU TO TAKE US TO WHERE YOU SPOTTED THE TWO MEN
BADGER WILL GO WITH YOU - AND DETECTIVE-SERGEANT CONNELL IS ANXIOUS TO START RIGHT AWAY
I HOPE WE GET THERE IN TIME TO CATCH THE SPIES
WE SAW THE SPIES FROM THERE
COME ON! QUIET AS CATS - AND KEEP YOUR HEADS DOWN!
LOOK - THERE'S ONE OF THEM
AND THE OTHER'S ON THE END OF THAT ROPE!
GRAB HIM, LADS!
THERE'S NO DANGER. WE'RE IN TIME, THANKS TO YOU TWO!
GOSH, WE'VE CAUGHT FOREIGN SPIES!

THESE TWO ARE SPIES, BUT THEY'RE NOT INTERESTED IN THE RADAR-STATION. THEY'RE EGG-THIEVES! THEY FOUND THE EYRIE OF A PAIR OF EAGLES - THE FIRST TO NEST IN NORTHUMBERLAND FOR MANY YEARS - AND WERE AFTER THE EGGS, PROBABLY WORTH A HUNDRED POUNDS EACH TO A COLLECTOR

EAGLES ARE PROTECTED BIRDS, SO THESE BRIGHT BOYS WILL BE CHARGED UNDER THE ACT. YOU GUIDES HAVE DONE A JOLLY GOOD JOB!
I RECKON THIS GIVES US A STRONG CASE FOR CALLING OURSELVES THE EAGLE PATROL!
HEAR, HEAR!
WE'LL SPEAK TO BEAVER ABOUT IT, STORMY

I HAVE BEEN GIVEN THE HONOUR OF RE-NAMING THE OWL PATROL THE EAGLES
UP, THE EAGLES!
HURRAH!
THE END

L.A.H.

by Jean Howard

Mother's not well and has gone back to bed,
So who is that getting the tea?
The table is laid and the butter is spread
By a Brownie whose name is—well, ME!

The washing-up's done and the toys put away,
And everything's tidy and neat;
When Daddy comes home at the end of the day
He'll want something tasty to eat.

Boil Mother an egg, then heat up the stew;
Bathtime for Jenny aged three;
When Mummy's not here there's so much to do
For a Brownie whose name is—well, ME!

THE NEW Brownie

A True Story by Dorothy Pearce

Modupe never carried her books and pencils to school in a case. She set off each morning with them perched on her head.

Modupe lived with her mother, Mrs. Adunle, and her two brothers, Fidelis and James, just outside Lagos, in Nigeria.

Each morning Mrs. Adunle went to market, with baby James sleeping comfortably on her back, the way Nigerian babies do. Fidelis, a sturdy boy of three, trotted at her side. In the market she sold bowls of peppery soup and balls of dumpling-like dough called fufu to eat with the soup.

Modupe helped her mother make the fufu each evening. It had to be pounded in a great wooden bowl with a long stick. Modupe and Mother sang a song as they pounded, almost dancing round the big bowl.

As the market was halfway to school, the whole family set off each morning together. As far as the market Modupe carried on her head the little stool on which Mother sat all day, as well as her school books. With baby James securely tied on her back, Mother balanced the big bowl of fufu balls on her head, while Fidelis proudly trotted behind with a pile of banana leaves on his head. In the market his job was to wrap each fufu ball in a banana leaf, ready for the customers. They were a merry party, laughing and talking and shouting to friends whom they met on the road.

After school Modupe went back to the market. Going home, she usually carried James on her back, for Mother often had

Each morning the whole family set off to market

to carry Fidelis, who was tired after a long day in the hot sun.

One day the school headmistress came to Modupe's class to tell them some good news.

"We have a new teacher who knows all about Brownie Guides. Tomorrow she will tell you what Brownie Guides are and about the Brownie Guide Pack she wants to run for you. She will be called Brown Owl, and you children will be the Brownie Guides. It is great fun and at the same time you will learn many useful things."

Modupe ran all the way to the market that afternoon to tell Mother the good news.

When Mother heard that Brownie Guides would be after school hours, she shook her head and told Modupe she would not be able to be a Brownie Guide as she had to help with the children when school finished.

Modupe was sad at this, but she knew Mother worked very hard to send her to school at all, so she tried not to show how disappointed she was.

Modupe was the only one in the class who was not a Brownie. Her friends teased her when she said she wasn't joining. Modupe pretended she wasn't interested in Brownies, so that they wouldn't think Mother was stopping her. All the same, the night of the first Brownie meeting she did wish she too was staying for it. She tried not to think about Brownies as she walked home with James asleep on her back.

Next day the others were full of tales of the lovely time they had had and all that Brown Owl had told them they would be doing. They laughed and called Modupe "a silly old stay-at-home".

Brown Owl heard them teasing Modupe. Next meeting she said she had an important thing to tell them, so they must hold a Pow-wow. She explained

In the Pow–wow Ring the Pack planned to help Modupe become a Brownie

that what they were going to talk about was a Brownie secret and mustn't be discussed anywhere else afterwards.

"I know Modupe would love to be a Brownie, but she can't be because she has to help with her brothers in the market each afternoon. So, you see, she is already doing a good turn each day without the fun of being a Brownie. We mustn't tease her, but must try to help her share our Brownie fun. Perhaps one day she'll be able to be a Brownie too."

The Brownies thought hard about this. Then the two new Sixers had an idea. They asked if they might teach Modupe Brownie work and games during playtime.

Brown Owl thought that would be splendid. "It is a very good idea to teach her; then she will be ready to join one day."

So the Sixers taught Modupe lots of Brownie work and played the new games with her in the playground.

Children in Nigeria, where it is very hot, mostly sleep on mats on the floor instead of in beds. One of the first things Brown Owl taught the Brownies was that it was important to air their bedmats each morning, then to roll them up instead of just leaving them on the ground.

Brown Owl taught them to air their bedmats

Mother thought this was a good thing when Modupe told her, so each morning Modupe hung the mats in the sun.

The Brownie Promise ceremony was fixed for the first meeting after the Easter holidays. Everyone was excited about it, but poor Modupe felt sadder than ever.

At the last meeting before the holidays the Sixers asked for a special Pow-wow.

"Please, Brown Owl, we've had another idea," one of them said. "If we went to the market in turn to help Mrs. Adunle, Modupe could come to the meeting and make her Promise with us."

Brown Owl was very pleased at this.

"I'll do something to help too," she said. "We'll have three extra meetings during the Easter holidays to make sure Modupe is ready to make her Promise."

"Will you tell her, Brown Owl?"

"I'd like you to, as it was your idea. Perhaps I'll come along with you too."

"After she's made her Promise, the whole Pack want to take turns with Modupe in helping Mrs. Adunle. That will only mean that each one will miss one meeting in fourteen, as there will be fourteen of us then."

"You have fixed everything well. I am proud of you," said Brown Owl, smiling.

Modupe was delighted when she heard the news. The Sixers went with her to tell her mother.

Mother was quite happy with the new plan.

"I did so want Modupe to be a Brownie, but I couldn't think of a way out. You're all very clever. It seems to me that Brown Owl has taught you a great deal in a short time. Thank you for finding a way for Modupe to join."

HOW BROWNIES BEGAN

A Rosebud wearing the early woollen cap

How many of you have older sisters? Quite a large number, I expect. Do you find that they can do all kinds of things that you'd love to do? Perhaps they are marvellous skaters or very good with horses. Perhaps they win cups for swimming or are excellent campers or shine at cooking, painting or gardening. Anyway, whatever it is that they enjoy doing, I expect that you too feel that you would like to have a try.

That's just how it was with younger sisters about sixty years ago. The older girls had started to be Guides and were doing a great many exciting things. Some of them learned how to travel like explorers over difficult country. If they came to a stream, instead of wasting time looking for a bridge which might be miles away, they would thrust their Guide pole or staff into the ground and swing themselves over. I wonder how many fell in when they were practising!

Some learned daring ways of rescuing people who might have become trapped in a burning house. Others knew just what to do if a horse became over-excited and galloped off wildly in a busy town; there were many horses in the streets in those days. Some felt they would like to be able to help injured soldiers and learned how to carry stretchers and to give first-aid.

Unfortunately, Guides were only for girls of eleven and over, and naturally there were thousands of under-elevens who also wanted to wear a uniform and prove themselves able to do brave and helpful things. Some of them turned up at the Guide meetings—but they were not invited and often got rather in the way! At last the grown-ups realised how much the under-elevens could learn and what a tremendous amount of help they could give and so a kind of Brownies was started. But they weren't called anything as interesting as Brownies! Their first name was quite different—Rosebuds!

The uniform was different too, for

the Rosebuds wore dark-blue blouses, skirts and caps, with brown belts and ties. Instead of your nice Brownie man in the trefoil, they had either a metal acorn or rosebud for their badge. On passing a test called Second Class they had an acorn with leaves, and for the First Class they added a motto to their badge.

Before Rosebuds made their Promise they had to know how to wash up and tie their ties. They also had to be able to plait their own hair, for nearly every girl had long hair in those days. Another thing they had to do was clean and fill salt-cellars. What would they have to be very careful about before they put the new salt in?

For their Second Class test they had to lay a table for four people and make a uniform tie or cap. They also learned how to tie up a parcel, to give first-aid, and to clean spoons, forks and knives. Knives had to be cleaned because people couldn't buy stainless ones as they can now.

The under-elevens liked the work and the games—but not the name. It didn't sound brave or energetic enough. All kinds of names were suggested, including Skylarks, Bantams, Buds and Bees. Then Lord Baden-Powell himself—the man who started Scouts and Guides—told us how in olden days many people believed there really were Brownie folk who crept secretly into homes where help was needed and did all kinds of useful jobs. So he felt that "Brownies"

Guides of fifty years ago practising first-aid

An early Brownie with straw hat — A Brownie of yesterday — A Brownie Guide of today

was the right name. It was some time later that the Six names of Sprites, Imps, Gnomes, etc., were thought of: at first the Sixes had the names of trees. Gradually the Brownies also changed their uniform. When I was a little girl, Brownies often wore straw hats. These were sometimes rather deep, with big curved brims, and often the Brownie looked as if she were peeping out from under a toadstool! Perhaps your grandmother wore one of these.

About sixty years ago there were just a few Brownies in Britain. Now there are thousands and *thousands* of Packs all over the world, in snow-covered lands and under tropical skics. They are all Brownies, and although like the early Rosebuds they may be different from you in some ways there's one way in which they are all alike, and always will be as long as there are Guides and Brownies. They've all made, as you have, a Promise to do their best and to help other people—and that, as you know, is what really makes a Brownie!

The Rosebud's Badge — The Brownie Man Badge — The Brownie Guide Promise Badge

WHERE DO THEY

SUSAN KING TELLS YOU IN WORDS AND PICTURES

You know that some birds fly away to the warm lands in autumn because our climate is too cold for them. What about the animals, though, who cannot escape from the frost and the snow that winter often brings?

Many of them are still about, of course, even in the coldest weather. You sometimes see their footprints in the snow. Others hibernate and go to sleep, making themselves as cosy and warm as possible until spring comes.

When the water in the ponds becomes too cold, it is time for the frogs to hibernate. They burrow their way down into the mud at the bottom, where they stay till spring. Then, when the water is warmer, they come out again, often making a lot of noise as they do so.

What about those busy insects the ants? Where do they go? They hibernate in enormous clusters, hundreds of them curled up together in their underground nest. As they sleep, the ants on the outside get cold and wriggle their way to the middle; the others make room for them. All the time, they are most careful to see that their queen is kept in the centre of the ball, where she will not feel cold.

Squirrels only partly hibernate. Their

GO IN WINTER?

nest is shaped like a dome, up among the branches of trees. Throughout autumn, these little animals busily collect nuts, which they bury in the ground or in the hollows of trees. They sleep quite a lot in the winter, but from time to time they will wake up and have a meal of nuts. Quite often, though, they forget where they have hidden their store!

An animal that looks rather like a very small squirrel is the dormouse. His winter nest is made of grass, dead leaves or moss and is found on the ground beneath piles of leaves or inside the hollow of a tree. With him in the nest will be his store of nuts and seeds, for if he wakes up he is sure to be hungry. After a quick meal he will go back to sleep, rolled up in a ball with his head bent down and his bushy tail wrapped right round his body.

It is not likely that you will see a hedgehog in the middle of winter, unless you happen to live in the country and accidentally come across his hideaway. These animals go to sleep curled up in a ball, and don't wake at all till the spring comes. All through the summer they eat and eat and grow really fat, for they have to last a very long time without food. Their winter nest may be in a hollow or perhaps under old tree roots or a bed of leaves.

A. Babington Suggests

Things to Make and Grow on the Brownie Road and Highway

A Mini Garden

Instead of a bunch of flowers for your mother on Mother's Day, why not make a little garden in a dish instead? It looks very pretty, and if watered carefully will last many weeks.

Choose a shallow dish, or a saucer would do. Fill it with soil, and pick out any pebbles or lumps. About two days before you wish to give the present, find small plants, such as ivy, primrose or crocus, in your garden or on a walk in the country. If you dig them up on your walk, only take little seedlings and not the wild flowers.

Put the plants carefully into your dish, making sure that the roots are right in the soil. Then press round gently with your fingers. If you can obtain some moss, put this on the bare parts; it will look much nicer. A small piece of rock will give variety to your arrangement.

When you are satisfied with your garden, put it in a cool place and water it sparingly.

After two days, the plants will really grow in the soil, and look natural. Your mother will be delighted with it.

An Easter Nest

Obtain a small shallow dish. Lightly grease the outside with vaseline.

Tear some newspaper into strips and press them over the vaseline until the dish is covered. Now brush some paste over this layer, then press another layer of strips over the paste. Repeat this about three times (paste, then newspaper) and then put it to dry in a warm place.

It will take at least a day to dry. When it is ready, insert a round-ended knife between the dish and the thick paper layer; and prise this off.

Trim the edges, and then paint it. When it is dry, put a little cotton-wool inside, and place some sweets with a little yellow chick on it. It would look pretty on the table on Easter Sunday, or you could give it away as a small present.

A Seed Picture

There are hundreds of different types of seeds, and if you collect some they can be made into a very interesting "picture". First of all, collect as many different varieties as possible. Here is a list of some of them: marrow, orange, acorn, sycamore and maple. You will also find a few grains of rice, sago and lentils useful. Collect some very thin twigs, too.

Obtain a piece of wood or hardboard. Ask a grown-up to help by giving the wood a thin coat of white shellac. This stops the wood soaking up the glue you will be using.

Now try out your design by placing the seeds on a sheet of plain paper. The seeds lend themselves well to "flower" designs, but you could perhaps copy your Six emblem.

Using a small pair of tweezers, lift up each seed and smear the back with a little glue. Place it on the piece of wood, and continue until the design is finished.

Leave it to dry for a day, without moving it. When it is dry, paint it over lightly with some clear varnish. This will make all the seeds glossy, giving it a pleasing appearance.

Stand it on a shelf, or fix two small hooks in the back of the picture and hang it on the wall.

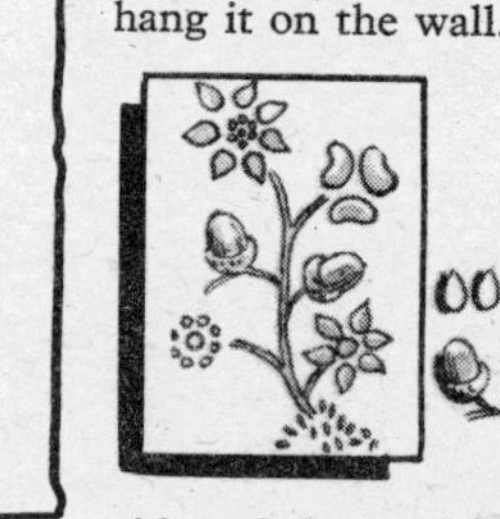

Bead Balls

You need a small plastic ball, small beads, glue and gold cord.

Make a hole with a large needle through the top and bottom of the ball.

Smear only the top half of the ball with stiff, strong glue. Press the beads on the glue, putting them close together.

Leave to dry. When ready, cover the rest of the ball with glue and complete the pattern. Leave to dry.

Thread a gold cord through the ball and hang on the Christmas tree.

Felt Medallions

You need scraps of felt, stiff paper, small beads (perhaps from a broken necklace) or sequins.

Cut out a circle of stiff paper, using a penny as a guide. Cut out two circles of felt the same size.

Place the paper circle between the felt circles, and oversew them together, using matching or contrasting silks or cotton.

Now sew the beads onto the medallion, scattering them, or making a simple pattern. Sew them onto both sides of the medallion, sewing through the paper. This is put in to make it stiff.

Sew a loop of thin cord to the top of the medallion, and hang it on the Christmas tree. Make as many as you like.

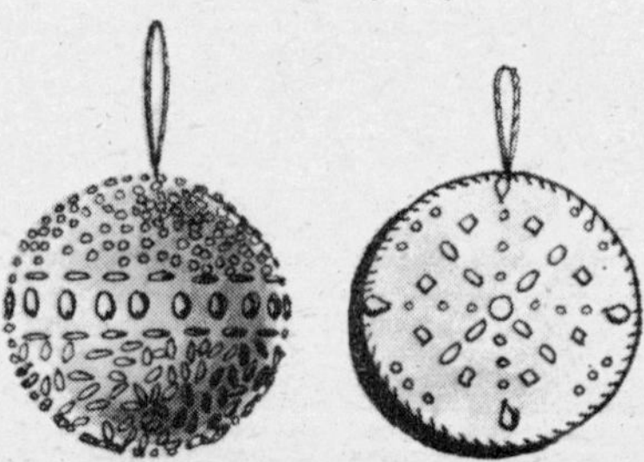

POTATO CUT PRINTING

GIRL GUIDES

FOR THE ARTIST BADGE (SECTION 2)

MAKE AN ALL-OVER DESIGN USING SOME METHOD OF PRINTING (POTATO CUT PRINT, HOME-MADE STICK PRINT) AND USE IT AS A BOOK COVER

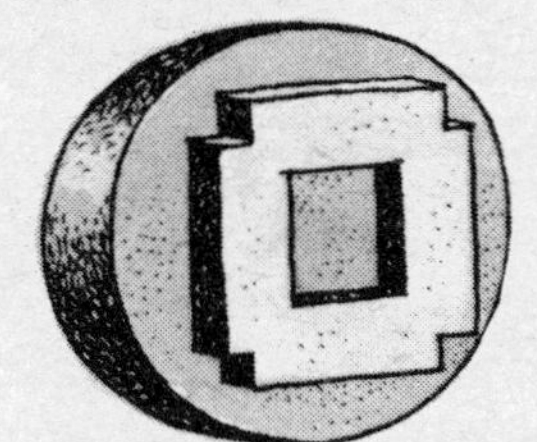

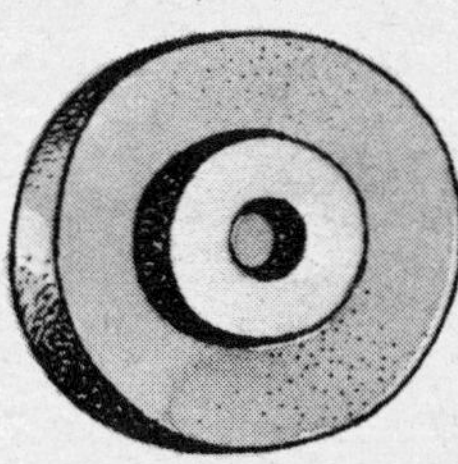

USE A NICE, FIRM, ROUND POTATO CUT IN HALF. WITH A SMALL PENKNIFE CUT ON THE LINES TO A ¼″ DEPTH

WITH THE POINT OF YOUR KNIFE CUT OUT THE BITS FROM THE SIDE. BE VERY CAREFUL ALWAYS TO CUT AWAY FROM YOURSELF

HERE ARE TWO MORE DESIGNS. USE SIMPLE SHAPES. YOU CAN MAKE ANY DESIGNS YOU THINK YOU CAN CUT CLEANLY.

YOU CAN PRINT IN BRIGHT COLOURS, USING POWDER PAINT WITH NOT TOO MUCH WATER. PAINT EVENLY ON TO THE POTATO WITH A GOOD BIG BRUSH

YOU CAN USE YOUR DIFFERENT DESIGNS LIKE THIS. USE A GOOD PIECE OF PAPER LARGE ENOUGH FOR THE BOOK COVER YOU WISH TO MAKE, ALLOWING ABOUT TWO INCHES ALL ROUND TO OVERLAP

NOW TO COVER YOUR BOOK

(1) PLACE THE BOOK WITH THE COVERS OPEN AS SHOWN, IN THE CENTRE OF THE PAPER. FOLD OVER AT (A) ONLY

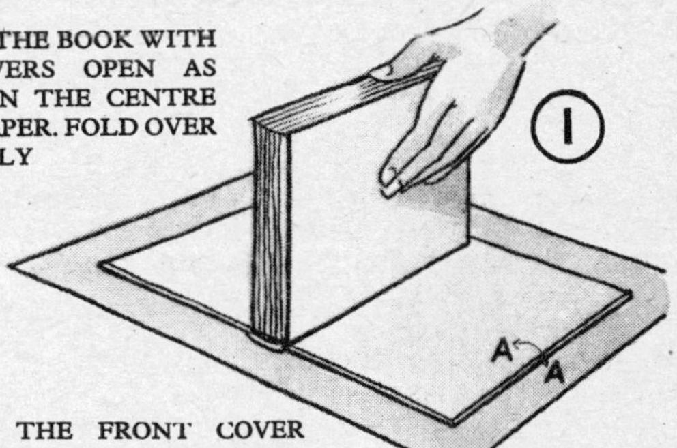

(2) CLOSING THE FRONT COVER (A), ALMOST CLOSE THE BACK COVER (B), PULL THE COVER TIGHTLY, TUCK IN, AND FOLD THE PAPER COVER OVER (C)

IF YOU FOLD OVER BOTH COVERS WITH THE BOOK WIDE OPEN, YOU WILL FIND IT WILL NOT CLOSE AS THE PAPER WILL BE TOO TIGHT.

NOW MAKE TWO SMALL CUTS AT (D)

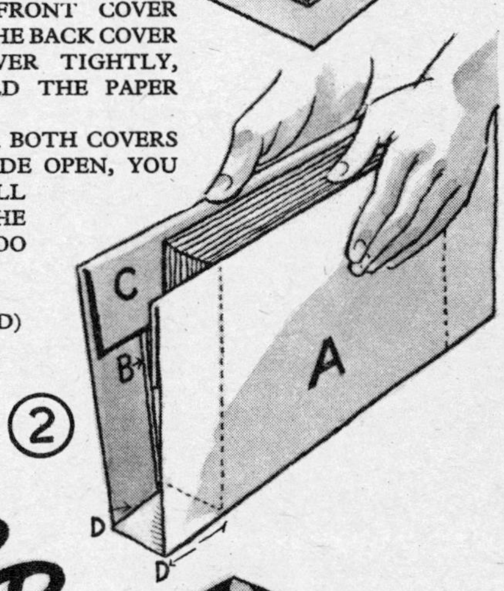

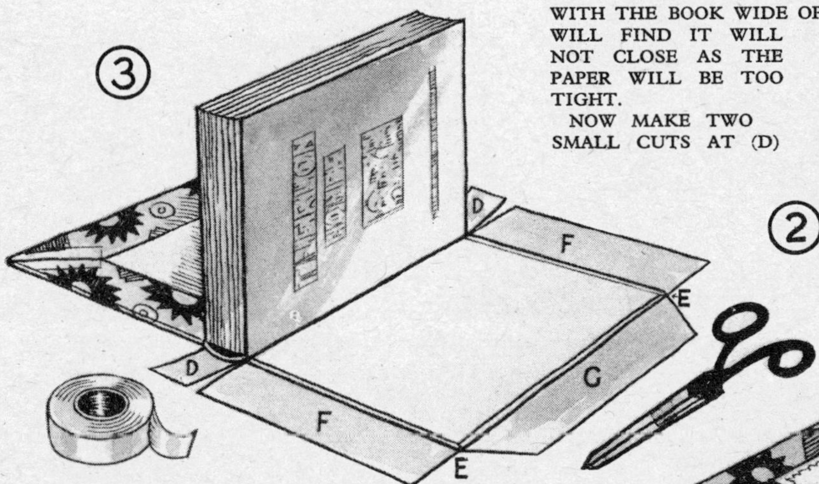

FOLD THE ENDS (F) OVER FIRST, THEN THE SIDES (G).

(3) OPEN OUT AND CUT THE OVERLAPS TO THE RIGHT SIZE UP TO THE CORNERS (E), TAPER THE ENDS OF THE TWO SIDE PIECES. INSERT AND STICK DOWN NEATLY WITH TRANSPARENT STICKY TAPE. THE SMALL PIECE (D) CAN BE TUCKED INSIDE THE BINDING

MAKE A NEAT LABEL SHOWING THE TITLE

POW-WOW RING IN STONE

THE EDITOR TELLS YOU ABOUT A STRANGE HAPPENING OF LONG AGO

Photos by Harry Hammond

Just think of it—sixty Brownies in a Pow-wow Ring suddenly turned to stone!

Don't be alarmed; it didn't really happen! But high up on the Cotswold Hills, not far from Stow-on-the-Wold, there is a strange stone circle thousands of years old that when I saw it made me think at once of Brownie Guides in a Pow-wow Ring. There are about sixty stones—exactly how many nobody knows, because they can't be counted—and they are of all shapes and sizes, just like Brownies! There are tall Brownies and short Brownies, stout, stumpy Brownies, and Brownies looking at you with heads on one side—except, of course, that they aren't Brownies, but soldiers, soldiers of long, long ago.

The story goes that an olden chieftain wanted to be king of England. So he gathered a small army about him and set forth to conquer. When he reached a hill near the Cotswold villages of Great and Little Rollright

"You and your men shall hoar stones be"

The King Stone

he was met by a witch, who told him to take "seven long strides" and then look down from the ridge.

"If Long Compton you can see
King of England you shall be,"
she promised.

Jubilant, the would-be king hurried on and up, calling out:-

"Stick, stock, stone,
As King of England I'll be known"

But the crafty old witch made a big mound rise up in front of him, and she cried out:-

"As Long Compton you cannot see,
King of England you shall not be.
Rise up, stick, and stand still, stone,
You and your men shall hoar stones be,
And I shall be an eldern tree."

The "king" and his men were turned to stone where they stood, and there they still stand, the "king" a little distance away by himself, his "soldiers" in a circle, and five "knights" who had hung back to plot against their leader in a field some distance away.

The stones are called the Rollright Stones, and they stand beside the road numbered A436, not far from the Oxford—Stratford-upon-Avon road (A34). They are said to be named Rollright after a Dane named Rollo, and some people think they were put up in that lonely place on the top of a hill to mark a victory in battle of Rollo. Others believe the stone circle to be the remains of a temple of the Druids, and there is no doubt that the Rollright Stones are as old or older than the famous stone circle at Stonehenge, where Druids are supposed to have had a temple for sun-worship.

I said earlier that the stones couldn't be counted. Well, the Brownies in the photographs all counted them—and each got a different answer! The Brownies are Patricia Charles, Cindy Smithers, Elizabeth Pixley, and Clare Blomfield, all of the 17th Cheltenham (Bethesda) Pack.

Once upon a time a baker thought of a way in which he could find out for certain how many stones there were. He filled a cart with loaves and carefully counted them. Then he set off for the Rollright Stones and placed a loaf on each stone. You'd think that when every stone had a loaf on it and he counted the number of loaves left in his cart he couldn't make a mistake, wouldn't you? Ah, but, you see, to his astonishment, he found he had used up all the loaves he had brought and there were still stones without a loaf! He just didn't know what to make of it. He leaned against one of the stones and scratched his head in perplexity. Then suddenly by the light of the moon he saw fairy fingers busily tipping his loaves from the top of the stones! Now he understood! He was

Four live Brownies and five stone Knights

"Forty-three, forty-four, forty-five. . . ." Elizabeth, Clare, Patricia and Cindy march round the stones and count as they go

up against the fairy folk, and they were playing tricks on him!

He didn't wait a minute longer. He picked up his loaves, tossed them back into his cart, and made off! He took care, though, to leave a nice new loaf in the middle of the circle for the fairies to feast on, just to make sure they wouldn't follow him and do him a mischief for intruding into their domain at midnight.

Perhaps, if you live near enough, your Guider would take you and your Pack to see the Rollright Stones, which, though not spectacular in themselves, are very interesting for the stories told about them. Perhaps you could make a Challenge to find out more about them, make a drawing of them, or write a new story about them, perhaps imagining how they came to be put there, and when, and why.

Be careful not to go there, though, at midnight! Do you know why? Well, there is a legend—that is, a folk-tale or fairy-tale—that every midnight all the stones rush down the hillside to drink at the stream at the bottom. You wouldn't want to be in their way when they did that, would you? —R.M.

"It's no use – every time we go round we get a different number"

After the Brownies' outing to the Rollright Stones, two Guides from a Cheltenham Company visited the circle. They are reading about it in this photograph. Afterwards they counted the stones – and, like the Brownies, got a different total each time!

JENNIFER BROWN

by
Edna Gilbert

1. Have you heard what happened
To Jennifer Brown,
The girl who was dreaded all over the town?

2. She never looked tidy,
Her hair was a fright,
And really her manners were far from right!

3. She'd tease girls and cheat them;
She'd steal and she'd lie.
She thought it was great fun
To make someone cry!

4. Some children are naughty
But nice with it, too.
Jennifer Brown was
Bad through and through!

5. Then something happened to Jennifer Brown,
Who smiles now and greets you
When she meets you in town.

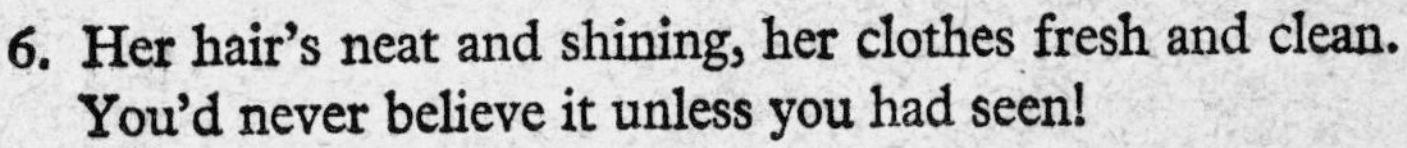

6. Her hair's neat and shining, her clothes fresh and clean.
You'd never believe it unless you had seen!

7. I met her one morning, and, strange to relate,
She carried my parcels right to the gate!

8. "Excuse me," I said, "but I would like to know
Whatever has happened to change you so?"

9. Then Jenny stopped smiling, though still her eyes shone.
She said, "I was hateful, but that has all gone!

10. For now I'm a Brownie, and proud as can be.
I'm thinking of *others*, instead of *me*!

11. I learned to be useful, make sad people smile.
It wasn't so easy just for a while.
But I knew I could make it.
I soon lost my fears,
And I've not been so happy
For years and YEARS!"

PLAYS WRITTEN BY BROWNIES

All these plays were written by Brownies in the Weybridge Division of West Surrey. They were entered in a competition for the best play by a Brownie. The winner received as a prize a lovely book, *The Challenge Book of Brownie Stories*, by Robert Moss, the Editor of the *Brownie Annual*, who judged the plays. Which did he think the best? Well, which do *you* like best? Read them and see; then turn to page 81 and see whether your choice was the winner.

THE TALKING FISHING ROD

***by Hilary Dooris,** 5th Chertsey Pack*

ACTORS

Peter (the fisherman)
Jane (his wife)
Tom (his son)
Tim (his son)
John (the fisherman)
Barbara (his wife)
Carole (his daughter)
Wendy (his daughter)
Mark (his son)
David (the fisherman)
Margaret (his wife)
Rod's voice
A Reader

ACT 1

READER: *One day, Peter, John and David the fishermen were out fishing. Tim, Tom and Mark were with them. They all had fishing rods as well. John was trying his fishing rod for the first time. He had only bought it that morning.*

JOHN: I say, Peter, this rod seems a good one or it's my lucky day. We have only been here forty minutes and I have just landed my twenty-ninth fish.

PETER: It's all right for some people. I have only landed eight so far.

DAVID: I have landed thirteen.

TIM: I haven't landed any.

TOM: Neither have I.

MARK: I have had one.

READER: *Just that minute Barbara came.*

BARBARA COMES ON TO THE STAGE.

JOHN: Hallo, what have you got?

BARBARA: I have got your tea. The others are coming.

WENDY COMES ON THE STAGE.

WENDY: How many have you caught, Daddy?

JOHN: I have caught thirty so far.

PETER: He's the luckiest.

DAVID: I agree.

JANE, CAROLE, MARGARET COME ON TO THE STAGE.

CAROLE: Who's caught the most?

DAVID: John has, of course.

READER: *Just then there was a voice*

ROD: It said "Quick, John, I have caught one for you."

JOHN: Who's speaking?

ROD: I said it.

JOHN: Who is I?

ROD: I said it and I am your rod.

JOHN FALLS BACKWARDS WITH SURPRISE.

JANE: For goodness' sake it's not that surprising.

MARGARET: You often hear of flying shoes.

JOHN: But you don't hear of talking fishing-rods.

CAROLE: Can we keep it a secret?

BARBARA: I would if I were you, John.

JOHN: All right, then.

MARK: Shall we give him a name?

TOM: I think Pluto suits him.

WENDY: Pluto sounds like blue and he is blue.

JOHN: All right. Pluto is his name.

TIM: We have got to tell him not to talk when people are near.

JOHN: (making sure no one is about): Rod, your name is going to to be Pluto.

PLUTO: Thank you very much. I like that name.

JOHN: Pluto, please don't talk when people are about.

PLUTO: All right, I won't.

PETER: I have caught eighteen now.

DAVID: I have only caught sixteen.

CAROLE: How many have you caught, Mark?

MARK: I have caught eight now.

TIM: I have caught five, so Mark has caught more than me.

TOM: I have only caught three.

PETER: I think you're all doing extremely well.

DAVID: I wasn't as good as you as a child or as lucky.

JANE: I think it's time we had tea.

TOM: I'm hungry.

MARGARET: Come on and have tea.

ALL SIT DOWN AND START EATING.

READER: *After tea they all went home. Pluto brought luck to John, Peter and David and they were the best fishermen in their district. They all lived happily ever after. When Mark, Tim and Tom grew up they were fishermen. Mark was given Pluto as a present and took his father's place as the best fisherman in the district and so it went on through the family.*

THE END

THE FOREST FIRE

by Hilary Dooris, *5th Chertsey Pack*

CHARACTERS

Mr. Mole
Mr. Dormouse
Mrs. Woodmouse
Woodcutter Jack
Mrs. Mole
Mr. Badger
Mr. Toad
Woodcutter Bill
Fire Brigade
John (the shoemaker)
Peter (his helper)
Suzie (his wife)
Don, Clive and Anne (friends)
A Reader

ACT

READER: *One day woodcutter Jack and woodcutter Bill were sitting by the camp fire in the forest. After breakfast they made the fire safe and went off to work.*

WOODCUTTERS GO OFF THE STAGE.
MR. AND MRS. MOLE COME ON.

MR. MOLE: Hurry up, deary.

MRS. MOLE: I'm coming.

MR. AND MRS. MOLE COME TO THE PLACE WHERE THE WOODCUTTERS HAVE BEEN.

MRS. MOLE: Oh! Look at that smouldering fire.

MR. MOLE: Isn't it dangerous.

MRS. MOLE GOES TO GET SOME FRIENDS.
MR. MOLE GUARDS THE FIRE.
MRS. MOLE COMES BACK.

MRS. MOLE: Here are our friends.

MR. DORMOUSE, MR. BADGER, MR. TOAD, MRS. WOODMOUSE ALL COME ON.

MR. BADGER: I suggest three people follow the woodcutters.

MR. TOAD: Very good idea, but who will go and who will stay.

MRS. WOODMOUSE: I would like to stay.

MRS. MOLE: So would I.

MR. MOLE: I will go as I know the way the woodcutters went.

MR. DORMOUSE: I would like to stay, and anyway I can't walk very fast.

MR. BADGER: Well, that settles it. Toad, will you come?

MR. TOAD: I will come with you.

MR. MOLE: We will start in a minute or two.

MR. BADGER: Let's get something to eat first.

MR. TOAD: I would like a drink, please.

MR. MOLE: I would like one too.

MR. BADGER: Let's get going. We will get a drink on the way.

MR. MOLE, MR. BADGER, MR. TOAD GO OFF STAGE.

MRS. MOLE: Does anyone think we could get the fire out?

MR. DORMOUSE: I don't think we could get it out, but we could try.

MRS. WOODMOUSE: I'll get some things to help put it out.

MRS. WOODMOUSE GOES OFF STAGE.

MRS. MOLE: I'll get some too.

MR. DORMOUSE: So will I.

MRS. MOLE AND MR. DORMOUSE GO OFF STAGE.

READER: *While they have gone the fire spreads. It spreads to the nearest part of the forest. It is still spreading when they all eventually get back with their things.*

MRS. MOLE, MRS. WOODMOUSE, MR. DORMOUSE COME BACK ON THE STAGE.

MRS. WOODMOUSE: Let's spread out.

MR. DORMOUSE: I'll go south.

MRS. MOLE: I'll go north.

MRS. WOODMOUSE: I'll stay here.

MR. DORMOUSE, MRS. WOODMOUSE, MRS. MOLE, ALL SEPARATE.
MR. MOLE, MR. TOAD, MR. BADGER ALL COME ON STAGE.

MR. BADGER: Oh! It's spread.

WOODCUTTERS COME ON THE STAGE.

JACK TO BILL: Bill, you didn't make the fire safe.

BILL TO JACK: I did, Jack.

JACK: Well, it doesn't look like it.

JACK AND BILL SET TO WORK TO GET THE FIRE OUT.

MR. BADGER: We had better keep out of the way.

ALL ANIMALS MOVE AWAY FROM THE FIRE.

BILL: Let's have a cup of tea. The fire is almost out.

JACK: Can't you wait a minute or two till it's fully out?

BILL: All right, then, but hurry up, please.

JACK: Why, while we have been talking it's begun to spread.

BILL: Well, do something, then.

JACK: I'll go south, you go north and work nearer, and run.

WOODCUTTERS SPREAD OUT SOUTH AND NORTH.

READER: *While they had gone the fire spread and spread everywhere, east, west, everywhere. The animals scampered from hiding and went to find some people. The fire spread and spread. Soon nearly the whole forest was on fire. After about half an hour the animals came scampering back.*

ANIMALS COME ON THE STAGE.

JOHN, SUZIE, PETER, ANNE, DON AND CLIVE COME ON THE STAGE WITH SOME BUCKETS OF WATER.

JOHN: Let's get to work. Don, take some water to Jack. He is in the south part of the forest. Peter, take some water to Bill in the north while I get the fire-brigade.

PETER, DON, JOHN, GO OFF THE STAGE.

ANNE: Let's start to put it out. We have a lot to do.

SUZIE: We certainly must start.

CLIVE: I agree with you, Suzie.

FIRE BRIGADE COME ON AND SET TO WORK NOW.

READER: *In about four hours the fire was finally out. Everyone was pleased and they all thanked the animals for telling them about the fire. As for them they lived happily ever after.*

THE END

THE WAGTAILS

by Heather Lawley
1st Ottershaw Pack

CHARACTERS
Willy Wagtail
Wilhelmina Wagtail
Baby Wagtail

Brownies: Margaret and Rosemary

DAYTIME

WILLY: I think we will have to teach our little baby to fly.

WILHELMINA: But, Willy, the baby ate too much when he hatched.

WILLY: I know, but he will be hopeless if he cannot fly.

WILHELMINA: Never mind, we will go and see Mr. Owl tonight.

EVENING

WILHELMINA: I am scared, Willy.

WILLY: Stay close to me, then.

WILHELMINA: I do not think that my idea was a very good one.

WILLY: Well, if you had not thought about it our baby might not be able to fly.

When they reached Mr. Owl's house he was out hunting, so they had to go back to their nest.

NEXT MORNING

Willy and Wilhelmina did not know that there were two Brownies watching them.

MARGARET: Oh, look! That little baby wagtail has something wrong with its wing.

ROSEMARY: Oh, good! The mummy and daddy wagtail have gone to fetch some food. Maybe we can fetch Brown Owl and she will tell us how to mend its wing.

MARGARET: Oh, look! The baby wagtail has fallen out of the nest. Quick, help me to catch it before it reaches the ground because the poor little wagtail will hurt its wing more.

The Brownies got Brown Owl and she showed them how to look after the wagtail till its wing was better. Wilhelmina did not worry about the baby wagtail because Margaret told her about Wilhelmina's baby. Later on in the week the baby was better and could fly.

WILHELMINA: Oh, Willy, I am so happy the Brownies were so helpful.

LATER AT BROWNIES

BROWN OWL: I am delighted to give Margaret and Rosemary their Animal Lover's Badge.

MARGARET: Oh, I am so happy because I had no pet to get my Animal Lover's Badge.

ROSEMARY: So am I.

EDITOR'S NOTE: ***To gain the Animal Lover badge, Margaret and Rosemary would have to do several other things – see your "Brownie Guide Handbook", page 111***

THE END

ANOTHER PET *by Wendy Morgan,* *5th Chertsey Pack*

CHARACTERS
Susie *Mum*
Wendy *Dad*

SUSIE: Over the week-end my guinea-pig had babies. Would you like one?

WENDY: Yes, please, but I will have to talk it over with Mum and Dad.

WENDY: Mum, Susie's guinea-pig has had babies and she asked me if I would like one. Could I have one, please?

MUM: I will have to talk it over with Dad. We will have to see about a cage.

MUM: Wendy has asked if she could have a guinea-pig.

DAD: We don't want a guinea-pig.

MUM: But Wendy would like one.

DAD: Does this mean we have got to make a cage?

MUM: We could always buy one. I wouldn't mind one.

MUM TO WENDY: Daddy says you can have one as long as you clean it out yourself.

WENDY TO SUSIE: Mum and Dad agree that I can have a guinea-pig.

THE END

THE OLD HOUSE

by ***Ann Susan Webbern,*** *2nd New Haw Pack*

ACT I

Four children have gone to stay with their aunt in a large house in the country. They are looking for a brown gate where their mother said the house would be

KITTY: I wonder where we are. This place is like a jungle.
LILY: Let's take that turning. It must lead to some sort of house.
EDWARD: It's a bit overgrown and there's a lot of brambles at the side of it.
PAUL: You're not scared, are you?
LILY: Well, if he is he can stay here and if we find our aunt's house we can come back for him.
EDWARD: Oh, no. It might be a long way from here and anyway you might forget me.
KITTY: Don't talk so much and let's see where this path goes to. It's getting dark.
The children make their way along the road until they come to a brown gate.
KITTY: It's a brown gate. We must be near.
PAUL: What's the matter, Lily?
LILY: Look, a house and it's ever so spooky.
EDWARD: It's a house. You're right, and it's got ivy all up it and one window is broken.
PAUL: Well, we must go in sooner or later.
The children go up to the house and Edward knocks.
LILY: I hope it's better looking inside.
The door opens and there stands a kind old woman.
AUNT: Hullo, do come in. You're late. The train arrived at 5 o'clock and it's long after that now.
PAUL: Well, we got lost on the way.
AUNT: Oh, I know. It's that path.
Aunt takes them to their rooms.
KITTY: My bed's very old.
LILY: So is mine.
PAUL: Let's not fuss and get some sleep. She's a nice old lady really and we can have a lot of fun here.
During the night the children heard some noises.
PAUL: Quick, pack your bags and let's go before our aunt finds out.
The children left the house and arrived at the station at 8 o'clock.
STATIONMASTER: What are you children doing here at this time of night?
LILY: Oh, we were scared.
PAUL: We will have double tickets, please.
The children get on the train.

THE END

THE LOST BADGE

by Julie New

2nd Weybridge Pack

BROWNIE JEAN: Oh dear, it's Brownies tonight and I can't find my badge.
MOTHER: Are you sure you looked in your cupboard well?
JEAN: I am sure, Mother.
MOTHER: Where could it be, then?
JEAN: I don't know!
MOTHER: Daddy will be coming home soon, so you'd better tell him you're not going to Brownies till you can find your badge.
JEAN: Father is home. I will tell him.
JEAN TOLD HIM
FATHER: The best thing to do is to stop and help look for the badge, because you are so proud of your badge.

SO THEY ALL HELPED
JEAN: (shouted out): I think I know where it is, in my wardrobe.
SHE LOOKED AND THERE IN THE LEFT POCKET OF HER UNIFORM WAS HER BADGE
FATHER: I should clean it extra special because you found it.
SHE WENT TO BROWNIES FEELING PROUD OF HERSELF. AND EVEN MORE PROUD WHEN SHE GOT A POINT FOR A NICE CLEAN BADGE. SHE TOLD BROWN OWL ALL ABOUT IT. BROWN OWL LAUGHED.

THE END

THE TWINS FIND A BOX

by Susan Daws and Rosemary Green

2nd New Haw Pack

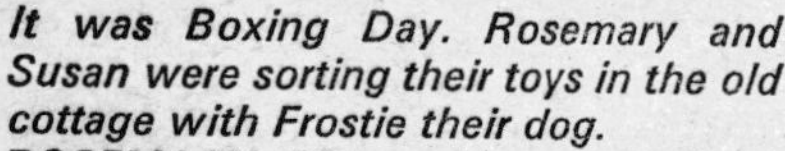

It was Boxing Day. Rosemary and Susan were sorting their toys in the old cottage with Frostie their dog.

ROSEMARY: Did you hear that noise?

SUSAN: Yes, it sounded like footsteps.

ROSEMARY: Let's go and find out what it was.

SO OFF THEY WENT

ROSEMARY: What's that brown thing over there?

SUSAN: I don't know—let's go and have a look.

ROSEMARY: Susan, Frostie, come quickly!

SUSAN: What is it?

ROSEMARY: It's a box with a key.

SUSAN: I am going to turn that key.

ROSEMARY: No, Susan — there might be something horrible inside.

SUSAN: I'm brave.

(AS SHE SAID THIS SHE TURNED THE KEY AND INSIDE FOUND NECKLACES AND WATCHES)

ROSEMARY: Ooh! What a find.

SUSAN: We had better go to the police station.

(WHEN THEY GOT THERE THEY TOLD THEIR STORY AND WERE TOLD THAT THERE WOULD BE A REWARD FOR THEIR FAMILY)

THE END

THE GIANT AND THE GNOME

by

Carol Lewis and Tonia Wise

4th Hersham Pack

SCENE ONE

JEREMY: Golly, isn't it hot today.

JULIA: Yes, it is hot *(wiping her brow).*

JULIA: Oh, here come our friends John and Mary. Now that we are here let's play something.

JOHN: I know, let's sing "The Sky is Blue."

ALL SING: The sky is clear, as clear can be,
Fiddle-la-la, Fiddle-le-le
The sun is shining for all of us,
Fiddle-la-la, Fiddle-le-le

REPEAT: So merry we are and merry we'll be
Fiddle-la-la, Fiddle-le-le

MARY: That really was fun. Oh, who is this? Why, I do believe it's a gnome.

GNOME: Why, it's a human child. I wonder if you could help me.

ALL: Why, of course we'll help.

GNOME: Oh, thank you very much indeed. You see, there's a horrible giant wanting to steal my apples.

JEREMY: Come on, then. What are we waiting for?

NARRATOR: *So they all ran off, only too willing to help the little gnome.*

SCENE TWO

JOHN: I'm puffed after that.

MARY: (scream). Oh, look. It's that horrid giant that gnome was telling us about.

JULIA: He's so ugly that I think I'll go home.

JEREMY: You'll do nothing of the sort. If we promised that we would get rid of the giant we will, including you. Now come on.

NARRATOR: *So they all troop off to meet the giant.*

JOHN: Hey, you, there. Don't you know that you're trespassing on to a gnome's land?

GIANT: What! Do you want me to leave these lovely apples?

JOHN: Yes, that's what I want you to do.

GIANT: My goodness, no! I will not leave these lovely apples.

NARRATOR: *Just then three little gnomes come tripping and skipping past the giant.*

GIANT: Hey, you little gnomes, Will you dance for me because I am so lonely?

NARRATOR: *So while those little gnomes danced for the giant the children got a sack each and collected as many apples as they could and then crept away.*

GIANT: Oh, I have been tricked! All those lovely apples have gone.

SCENE THREE

GNOME: Oh, thank you so much. You have saved my apples and now as a reward we will all eat apple pie.

NARRATOR: ***So they all feasted on apple pie till they could eat no more and the giant went away and did not trouble the little gnome any more.***

IT HAPPENED AT THE CASTLE

by Penelope Gowan and Monica Gray *2nd New Haw Pack*

CAST

Brownies Kathy, Suzey, Alison and Rosemary.
Pack Brown Owl.
Robber.
Mrs. Wheeler.
Policemen, Inspector.

BROWN OWL: Everybody come and sit down in a circle, please. It's such a nice evening that I thought we would have the meeting outside. Rosemary, go and get the box from the shed, please.
ROSEMARY: Yes, Brown Owl.
ALISON: Oh, hello, Mrs. Wheeler, we thought you weren't coming. It's a quarter past six. Here you are, sit here; you said you liked to sit in view of the front of the castle.
MRS. WHEELER: Oh, thank you, dear. I'm sorry I'm late, but something awful has happened.
KATHY: What, Mrs. Wheeler? Do tell us.
MRS. WHEELER: Someone has stolen my beautiful vase which my

great-aunt had given me and my gold chain and my silver box which my mother gave me.
ROSEMARY: Here's the box, Brown Owl, but I found this in the corner of the shed.
BROWN OWL: What is it?
SUZEY: What, a sack?
ROSEMARY: Yes, I think there is something inside.
SUZEY: Let's look inside. May we, Brown Owl?
BROWN OWL: All right, but someone will have to phone the police if it looks as if it's something that has been stolen. Rosemary, open it carefully in case there's something valuable inside.
(ROSEMARY OPENS IT)
MRS. WHEELER: Why, they're mine, my missing belongings.
ALISON: Yes, Brown Owl. Come on, Suzey. We'll phone the police.
(WHEN THE POLICE COME)
KATHY: Look at that man running down the hill.
INSPECTOR: Where, miss?
KATHY: Over there.
THE INSPECTOR: Oh, yes. Johnson and Silverton, chase him. Peterson and Brown drive around to the other side of the hill and help the others.
THE POLICEMEN: Yes, sir.
(QUARTER OF AN HOUR LATER)
THE POLICEMEN: We have caught him, sir. He's on the way to the police station.
THE INSPECTOR: The Pack will have a reward of a little sum of money.
BROWN OWL: Thank you, but let's finish our Pow-wow, Pack, before you go home because the time has been used for this venture.
MRS. WHEELER: Now I can go home and take my missing treasures with me. I just don't know what would have happened if you Brownies hadn't invited me to your meeting.
ALISON: That's all right, Mrs. Wheeler. The Brownie motto is Lend a Hand.

THE END

BETTY'S CAKE

by Diane Whitlock

5th Chertsey Pack

Once upon a time there was a little girl called Betty. Betty lived in the country.
BETTY: Please can I make a cake?
MOTHER: Yes, of course, dear.
BETTY: Where's the recipe book?
MOTHER: The usual place in the pantry.
BETTY: Is there any caster sugar?
MOTHER: I expect so.
BETTY STANDS ON TIPTOES TO REACH. SHE GETS ALL THE INGREDIENTS AND PUTS THEM IN A BOWL, STIRRING GENTLY, GETTING FASTER AND FASTER.
MOTHER: We can have the cake for tea.
BETTY: Goody. Can we keep it for a surprise?
MOTHER: Yes, hide it quickly. Here comes Father.
BETTY: Where shall I hide it?
MOTHER: Under the table.
IN WALKS FATHER.
FATHER: Hallo, everybody. Is dinner ready?
MOTHER: Nearly.
BETTY: Dinner's late today. It is nearly a quarter to two.
FATHER: How time flies.
MOTHER: Dinner's ready.
There was mashed potatoes and sausages for dinner and jelly for pudding. After dinner Father went to work again.
At last it was tea time. Proudly Betty brought out her cake. Father was to be the first to taste it.
FATHER: Ugh, how awful!
MOTHER: What's the matter?
FATHER: It's awful.
MOTHER: Let me taste it. Ugh, you must have put salt instead of sugar.
Betty was very sad her cake hadn't turned out after all.
MOTHER: Never mind. We can make another cake tomorrow and then we can ice it.

WIDE-AWAKE WENDY

by Jean Howard

It was a cold, wet evening in October. The lights from the shops shone on the rainwashed pavements and lit up the large pools of water that lay in the gutters and spread themselves across the shiny wet road.

Wendy tripped and fell against a shop door, which swung open

Wendy hurried along the High Street on her way home from school, her hood over her head and her hands thrust deep down into her mackintosh pockets.

Today she hardly noticed the bright lights and the busy crowds; even the rain on her face was just one more misery at the end of a really horrible day.

First she had overslept and been late for school. Then her pencil-case had disappeared from her desk; after much searching, she found that someone had borrowed it and forgotten to put it back again, so she only had time to do three sums before the bell rang.

The next lesson was reading, her worst subject. Everyone else was on book two or three whereas she was only on book one! As soon as she opened it, Susan Brace said, "Are you still on that old book?" then turned and whispered something to her neighbour, and they laughed unkindly.

The children were all expected to read in turn. When Wendy's turn came, she paused even longer than usual when she came to the word "spread", and everyone seemed to be getting more and more restless. Suddenly Susan's voice cut into the silence: "Please can we go on to Katie? Wendy is so slow; the bell is sure to go before we have all had a chance to read."

Miss Davis usually told Susan to be quiet, but today even she seemed to be getting rather cross. When Wendy stopped longer than ever over the word "bough" she snapped, "Really, Wendy, you're nearly nine years old. You certainly can't have done any practice at home. If you haven't improved by next week you will be on detention!"

Poor Wendy sat with her face burning and her eyes smarting with tears. Helen Gray, her Sixer in the Brownie Pack to which she belonged, turned round and whispered "Cheer up!", which helped a lot, and she got through the lesson.

At lunchtime, though, Wendy could hardly eat a thing. She kept thinking about the threatened detention! It was bad enough to be kept in after school, but supposing it meant missing Brownies too! She really did try to practise reading at home, but with a younger sister and twin baby brothers it was very difficult, and Mother was always so busy. No wonder she found salt tears mixing with the rain-drops on her face as she made her way home through the bustling crowds.

As she pulled her hand from her pocket to brush away the tears, she tripped over a rough piece of pavement and fell against a door. This could not have been quite closed, because it swung open, and Wendy found herself sitting on the floor of a small shop, surrounded by children's books of every sort and size.

A kind-looking lady came forward to see if she was all right, and she was so sympathetic when she saw Wendy's tear-stained face that suddenly the whole story of the reading lesson came tumbling out.

"Well," said the bookshop lady, with a smile, "you've come to the right place, haven't you? Actually, I need someone to help tidy up the books at the end of the day. You say you are a Brownie, and I know that Brownies are very helpful people, so ask your mother if you can stop by on your way home each day. When we've put the books back in their places you can sit on that little red stool and read till I'm ready, and then we can go home together."

Wendy could hardly believe her ears, but the bookshop lady kept her promise, and each day there was an exciting reading book waiting on the little red stool. Gradually the words began to make their own special pictures, and Wendy came to recognise them without having to spell them out every time.

At the next reading lesson the teacher, Miss Davis, looked rather surprised and said, "That's better, Wendy," and said nothing more about detention.

Wendy was determined to read really well by the end of the term. Every evening she went to the bookshop, and she practised reading all the advertisements on hoardings and in shops—even the names on vans and lorries waiting at traffic lights.

One dark-blue van she looked at had a very difficult name on its side. It was *EBENEZER DREWERSTONE & SONS, ELECTRICAL EXPERTS.* It was often parked outside the school, where the central heating was being repaired. Each day Wendy tried to work out what it said, but in the end Helen had to help her.

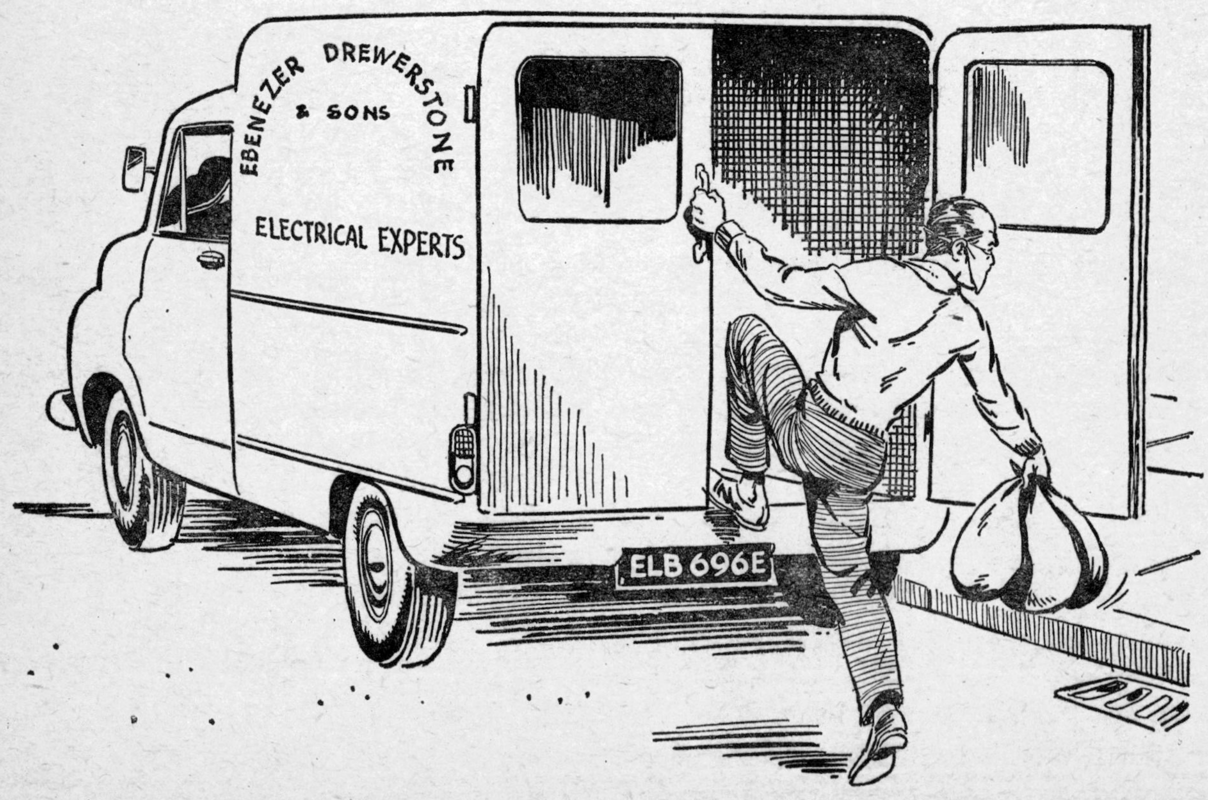

On the Saturday morning of the half-term holiday weekend, she was passing the Western Bank on her way to the bookshop when she saw the *EBENEZER DREWERSTONE* van outside. She amused herself by counting the number of "e's" in the words on the side; then, glancing at the number-plate, she noticed that this was ELB 696E. "That's funny—more E's", she thought. Perhaps the driver's name was Ernest! She looked at him to see if he looked like an "Ernest". He was sitting there biting his nails, and she didn't think he'd be likely to have the name Ernest. He wasn't the usual driver.

Hardly twenty paces on past the bank, she heard a scream, followed by shouting. She swung round and saw two masked men run out of the bank carrying several large bags. They jumped into the waiting van.

A young clerk chased them and grabbed one of the men as he tried to close the doors. There was a struggle, but he was pushed off backwards into the roadway and the van drove off at full speed down a side street and disappeared. The clerk did manage to hold on to one of the money bags, the contents of which spilled out into the gutter as he fell.

It all happened so quickly that Wendy could hardly believe her eyes. Only the sight of the poor bank clerk lying in the road, and the money scattered in all directions, convinced her that a raid had really taken place.

The rest of the bank staff rushed out. A crowd quickly collected. Within a few minutes the police arrived. The young man was helped to his feet, but he seemed too dazed to be able to speak. Suddenly Wendy realised that perhaps she was the

Wendy swung round in time to see two masked men run to the waiting van

only one able to identify the van.

Her legs felt very wobbly as she pushed through the crowd and went up to one of the policemen. She pulled at his sleeve, and said, "Please, I saw the van."

"Yes, all right, missy! Now run along home," said the policeman kindly.

"I mean I saw the number, and I've often seen the van outside the school."

The policeman looked at her intently. "Do you really mean that? Tell me quickly—what was it?"

Trying to remember all that Brown Owl had told her about giving a message clearly, she said, "It was a dark-blue van, with 'Ebenezer Drewerstone' on the side, and the number was ELB 696E. I know because I was counting the number of 'e's'. I often read number-plates to see if the letters make a word."

The policeman acted very swiftly. He used his walkie-talkie radio to send a message to all police patrol cars telling them to look out for the van with the name and number Wendy had given and arrest the men inside.

Within an hour the robbers were caught on their way to the coast. The money and the van were soon returned to their rightful owners.

The next week, at Brownies, Brown Owl said they were all very proud of the way Wendy had acted. She had been quick and sensible; the way she had learned to read so much better showed how hard she had worked. Now that she could read quite well, she would be the Second of her Six when Gillian left.

"You've certainly proved that you're a wide-awake Brownie, Wendy," said Brown Owl.

The bookshop lady also had a surprise for Wendy. When Wendy went there on the Monday afternoon, there was a parcel with her name on it on the little red stool, and inside was the *Brownie Annual*.

THIS IS THE LAW

Be sure that you know the Brownie Guide Law, which is: A BROWNIE GUIDE THINKS OF OTHERS BEFORE HERSELF AND DOES A GOOD TURN EVERY DAY. Then you won't make the mistake of a new recruit to a London Pack, whose idea of the Law was: A BROWNIE GUIDE ALWAYS HELPS HERSELF AND HAS A GOOD TIME EVERY DAY.

QUICK QUIZ

Set by Jean Howard

1. What colour are the *Brownie Pocket Books*?
2. How much does the *Brownie Guide Handbook* cost?
3. Which way does the cross of St. Andrew go on the Union Flag?
4. Name four badges beginning with "A".
5. What is the letter "R" in semaphore?
6. What sort of roof has your hall or meeting-place?
7. What is the largest creature in the world?
8. Where are the headquarters of the Girl Guides Association?
9. Describe your Brownie Guider's tie.
10. What games did you play two weeks ago?

BROWNIE HOUSE CROSSWORD PUZZLE

by

Brenda Morton

CLUES ACROSS

1. You don't need this round your neck at meals (3)
3. Drink from this (3)
5. Some of these have been seen flying (7)
6. For curtains or for catching fish in (3)
7. A toddler's plaything (3)

CLUES DOWN

1. You need this when cooking (5)
2. A knife shouldn't be this (5)
3. Holds blankets or treasure (5)
4. Pet name for a cat (5)

QUICK QUIZ

(page 60)

ANSWERS

1. No. 1–green; No. 2–red; No. 3–brown; No. 4–blue.
2. Five shillings (25 p.)
3. Diagonally. It's a white cross on a blue background.
4. Agility, Animal Lover, Artist, Athlete.
5. Both arms straight out from shoulders.
6. Check your answer at your next Pack meeting.
7. The whale.
8. 17–19 Buckingham Palace Road, London, S.W.1. It's called, for short, CHQ, meaning Commonwealth Headquarters.
9. Dark-blue crossover ribbon, two gold stripes.
10. Check with your friends whether you were right.

MAKE A WRIST PINCUSHION

M. I. ECKHARDT Shows You How

MATERIALS REQUIRED:
Two 4″ squares of material, such as felt, velvet or crimplene; a 4″ piece of thin elastic; 1 yard of lace (any colour); foam for filling; needle, cotton and scissors.

Cut the material into two circular pieces, diameter 4″. Take one piece of material and the lace. Tack the lace onto the WRONG side of the material, pleating it occasionally to give a frilled effect (Fig. 1).

Sew the two circular pieces together, RIGHT sides together, leaving a 1″ opening. Backstitch carefully all the way round, or sew on a sewing machine. Turn the pincushion the right way round and then fill with foam (a whole piece of foam makes a better filling than several little pieces). Carefully sew up the gap left for the filling, then sew the elastic on the back so that it can be worn on the wrist (Fig. 2).

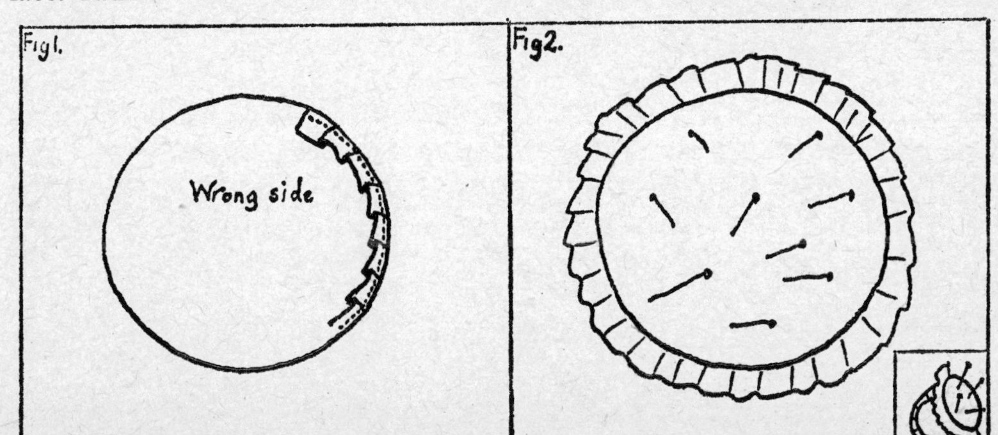

Wrist Pincushion

POST THAT LITTER!

by Jean Howard

1. Five excited Brownies
 Had a picnic with the Pack;
 Belinda ate an orange,
 Threw the peel behind her back.

2. Susannah had some chocolate.
 Gave Virginia a bit;
 They tossed the silver paper
 Into a sandy pit.

3. Miranda had some biscuits
 And some chocolate wafers, which
 She shared with Pam and Linda;
 Dropped the paper in a ditch!

4. Then Brown Owl saw the paper,
 Said they'd quite disgraced the Pack;
 So now they put their litter
 In the proper rubbish sack.

Good Turns

Among the many interesting items that appear each week in your own magazine *The Brownie* are letters from Brownies telling about Pack Ventures, good turns, outings, and the like. Here are two of the good turns reported. Congratulations, 1st East Barnet, and very well done, Teresa!

From Elizabeth Fletcher of the 1st East Barnet Pack, Herts.: We called our Pack Venture the BROWNIE TOADSTOOL FAIR, and here it is. By the time we had set up all the sideshows the people had already arrived. First we had the recorders playing their tune, and then we had a country dance in which every Brownie joined. This was followed by the play, and last of all came the jolly minstrel band. Afterwards everyone had a go on the sideshows, and people had refreshment, which were tea, orange or lemon, and cake and biscuits. The money amounted to £13, and we decided to spend it on a Pack good turn.

From the Brownie Guider of the 1st Marlow Pack, Bucks.: Teresa Treadwell, of this Pack, got up very early one morning, at 4 o'clock, and helped to make tea for firemen who were fighting a blaze at a chemical store near her home.

What is a Good Turn? asks the Editor

Good turns are not always *actions*, like helping an elderly lady across the road, but quiet deeds of thoughtfulness and kindness that no one would notice were "good turns" – like speaking to the lonely girl in the playground, asking the disliked girl to join in your play, calling for the friendless girl on the way to Pack meeting.

Several times when out with Brownies for photography for the *Brownie Annual* I've been the recipient of quiet, considerate "good turns". Once, on a very hot day at Chessington Zoo, I felt a tug on my arm and turned to find one of the Brownies holding out a choc ice to me. She'd bought it for me, unprompted, with her own money. I did enjoy that ice!

On another occasion, the Brownies ran into a shop to buy sweets. One of them came back with a bar of toffee for me.

Yes, good turns are often those "little, nameless, unremembered acts of kindness and of love" spoken of by the poet Wordsworth. "Unremembered"? I'd rather say never forgotten!

R.M.

Here's How to Make

A PRETTY SEASHELL PICTURE

by

Susan King

If you went to the seaside in the summer and collected some sea-shells, you may be wondering what to do with them.

Instead of leaving them in a box or in a paper bag, why not make a picture with them and hang it on the wall where everyone can see it? It might make a nice addition to your Six home.

You will need a piece of hardwood or fibreboard (your father may have a spare piece); a very thick piece of cardboard will do. A good size is 10 in. by 10 in., but you can have it smaller or larger than this.

Now to paint it. If your parents have been decorating your house they may very well have some emulsion or gloss paint you could use. Choose a really bright colour—a blue, for instance—so that your shells will stand out against a strong background.

While you are waiting for the paint to dry on your board, have a look at your shells and choose the best ones. Pick different shapes, colours and sizes. Then, after scrubbing them gently, arrange them in different ways until you find the arrangement you like best.

Now stick each shell carefully onto your dry board. You will need a really strong, quick-drying glue for this. Balsa cement is the best; it costs a few pence a tube. If you have a brother who makes models, he probably uses this type, anyway.

Read the directions on the tube container before starting; you will need only a small amount all around the edge of each shell.

Now you have finished, and you have an attractive reminder of your days at the seaside!

M.I. ECKHARDT SHOWS YOU HOW TO MAKE

AN INDOOR GARDEN

You will need an egg carton for half a dozen eggs, mustard-and-cress seeds, cotton-wool, paints, scissors and water.

Carefully cut off the lid of the egg carton. Paint the carton in bright colours. Paint M for mustard and C for cress as a pattern on top when dry. Half fill each section with cotton-wool, then wet with water.

Open your packets of seed and sprinkle some of the cress seeds into three of the sections. If you want both types of seed to grow at the same time it is better to sow the mustard seeds four days later.

Water the cotton-wool whenever it is dry, but not too much or it may soak into your carton and spoil it.

The seeds will soon grow. When they have grown to about 1½ inches high, snip them off with the scissors.

Now you can take your mustard-and-cress garden to Pack meeting, and then make yourself a tasty sandwich of mustard-and-cress.

Make Sure Your Parcel Arrives in One Piece

LEARN TO DO A PACKER'S KNOT

Debbie's parcel came to pieces—oh, what a mess!

Study pages 105–107 of the *Brownie Guide Handbook*

UNION FLAG PUZZLE

by Brenda Morton

Answer each clue with the name of a country or saint whose cross appears in the Union Flag.

1. Name of country whose saint was a Roman soldier
2. Saint who was a disciple of Jesus.
3. Country that has the thistle as its emblem.
4. Saint who was a bishop.
5. This saint was born in Cappadocia.

Who Was St. Swithin?

St. Swithin was buried in Winchester Cathedral on July 15th, 971, and it is said that it rained then and for forty days afterwards. People said it rained so much because St. Swithin had said he would rather be buried in the churchyard than in the Cathedral. Ever since then people have believed that if it rains on St. Swithin's Day it will rain for forty days.

St. Swithin's Day, if thou dost rain,
For forty days it will remain.
St. Swithin's Day, if thou be fair,
For forty days 'twill rain no more.

St. Swithin was an English bishop who lived about a thousand years ago. All kinds of stories were told about him. Here is an old rhyme that tells one of them:-

A woman having broke her eggs
By stumbling at another's legs,
For which she made a woeful cry,
St. Swithin chanced for to come by,
Who made them all as sound or more
Than ever they were before.
But whether this were so or no
'Tis more than you or I do know.

All Hallowe'en

Heyho for Hallowe'en,
When all the witches are to be seen,
Some in black and some in green—
Heyho for Hallowe'en.

All Hallowe'en is the last day of October and it means the eve of All Souls' Day. It is a day of great fun and merriment, especially in Scotland. In days long ago it was thought that witches could be seen on this night. Children might perhaps rather want to see a witch and yet be just a wee bit scared, as it seems was the little girl in this funny old rhyme:

Soul! Soul! for an apple or two.
If you've got no apples pears will do.
Up with the kettle and down with your pan;
Give me a good big one and I'll be gone!

All Hallowe'en is a day on which you *must* eat apples and nuts! Children used to go round asking for them on this day by reciting verses such as these:

This is old Hollantide night:
The moon shines fair and bright.
I went to the well and drank my fill.
On the way coming back
I met a pole cat:
The cat began to grin and I began to run.

It is said that if there is frost on Hallowe'en the weather will be mild at Christmas. Here is a funny rhyme about this:

If ducks do slide at Hollantide
At Christmas they will swim.
If ducks do swim at Hollantide
At Christmas they will slide.

DILYS AND THE DUCKLING

by Jean Howard

Dilys tried to catch the duckling, but it ran lopsidedly away to the water

Dilys was taking a short cut along the river-bank on her way home from school. She was hurrying because it was Brownies tonight, and she wanted to finish her homework before changing into uniform.

The Brownies were having a special meeting tonight, because it was the Pack's twentieth birthday, and they had invited the local Cub Scout Pack to join in their celebrations.

There was a cold east wind blowing, and the towpath was deserted except for a large family of ducks who crossed the road, slithered down the steep bank and plopped into the dark-grey water.

Dilys was just about to walk on, after watching the stately procession, when she noticed one little fellow trying to catch up with the rest of the family. He seemed to have difficulty in walking across the sandy path. When she looked more closely she saw to her horror that he had become entangled in a length of fishing line! He must have snapped at a fisherman's fly. His head was being pulled sideways by a piece of line which had caught round his beak and then twisted over his back and round one leg. He looked in a very sorry state.

Dilys tried to catch him, but he took fright and hurtled in ungainly fashion down the steep bank and into the water, where, in a lopsided way, he endeavoured to swim after the others, his head permanently turned towards the bank.

Suddenly Dilys remembered a quaint little prayer she had once read in a book, and she quoted it softly to herself.

"Dear God, protect all folk
who quack and everyone who
knows how to swim—Amen."

Although she knew that unless she hurried on she would be late for Brownies, Dilys couldn't ignore the duckling's plight. Perhaps she could be God's means of protecting this little quacking creature! She hurried back to a telephone kiosk and dialled the number of the local R.S.P.C.A. She had a sixpenny piece in her pocket.

On making the connection, she put her sixpence in the slot and described what she had seen on the river-bank. The R.S.P.C.A. inspector asked if she would wait on the bank until he arrived so that she could show him where to find the unfortunate duckling, so she ran back down the towpath and was just in time to see the family of ducks disappear under a willow-tree.

She had a cold, lonely vigil, but after about ten minutes a Land-Rover approached with an R.S.P.C.A. inspector and another man in it. Dilys ran up to the Land-Rover and made herself known to the R.S.P.C.A. inspector. The inspector told her they had brought a rubber dinghy. This they launched from a small sandy bay, and paddled down to the willow-tree.

As they moved in towards the bank, parting the branches carefully, the ducks swam swiftly out into the stream and away, but the handicapped duckling was unable to follow and went round and round in circles. After several unsuccessful attempts, the R.S.P.C.A. men finally caught him and gently disentangled him from the line.

Dilys watched from the bank. To her delight, the duckling seemed to be unharmed, for as soon as he was put back in the water he swam happily off.

Although Dilys was taken home in the Land-Rover, she arrived nearly an hour late at Brownies. Fortunately a rather late start had been made, so there was still time for her to join in the fun.

She told Miss Baily, the Guider, why she was late.

"I wish more people would help birds and animals when they see them in distress," said Miss Baily. "Well done, Dilys! We'll look on your own action as a very nice twentieth birthday present for the Pack!"

WASHDAY GOOD TURN

by Jean Howard

Snap, went the line;
Dropped the clothes on the ground;
All the clean sheets in a mess.
Two helpful Brownies
Soon pick them all up—
Shirts, towels, socks and a dress.

They soon put them back
In some warm soapy suds;
Now they're clean once again.
Mend the line with a knot
That the Brownies are taught,
And everything's soon right as rain!

THE OLD WELL

Story in Pictures by MERRIL BROWN

PUSS! PUSS!

I CAN'T SEE ANYTHING, BUT THERE IS A CAT DOWN THERE.

MIAOW!

LOOK, HERE'S A BUCKET. IF WE LET IT DOWN, THE CAT MIGHT GET INTO IT.

OH, I DO HOPE IT WILL HAVE THE SENSE TO GET IN, SUSAN!

BUT ALTHOUGH THE BROWNIES LET THE BUCKET DOWN AGAIN AND AGAIN, IT CAME UP EMPTY

IT DOESN'T UNDERSTAND THAT IT'S GOT TO GET IN, OR IT CAN'T GET IN, I EXPECT IT'S ONLY A KITTEN. OH, DEAR. IT WILL DIE IF IT STAYS DOWN THERE.

I'M GOING DOWN IN THE BUCKET, JENNIFER. IT'S STRONG ENOUGH TO BEAR MY WEIGHT.

WIND ME DOWN SLOWLY, JENNIFER.

OH, I'M SCARED! BE VERY CAREFUL, SUSAN.

10
OH, YOU POOR LITTLE PUSSY!
MIAOW!
ARE YOU ALL RIGHT, SUSAN?
11
I'VE GOT HIM, JENNIFER! HE'S ONLY A KITTEN.
THANK GOODNESS YOU'RE SAFE, SUSAN! I'VE BEEN SO SCARED.
12
PLEASE, DOES THIS KITTEN BELONG TO YOU?
HE WAS DOWN THE OLD WELL, AND SUSAN FETCHED HIM UP.
WHY, IT'S OUR THOMAS! HOW BRAVE OF YOU TO RESCUE HIM! HE'S A VALUABLE KITTEN, BUT HE'S ALWAYS GETTING INTO MISCHIEF.
13
WILL YOU PLEASE ACCEPT A BASKET OF BROWN EGGS AS A THANK-YOU FROM THOMAS AND ME FOR YOUR GOOD TURN?
THANK YOU VERY MUCH.
I'LL HAVE ONE FOR MY BREAKFAST.
14
I'VE JUST HAD A WONDERFUL IDEA FOR THE ELVES AT THE PACK FETE, JENNIFER. LISTEN .....

AT THE NEXT PACK MEETING...
15
WE'VE HAD SOME QUITE GOOD IDEAS FROM ALL THE SIXES EXCEPT THE ELVES. NOW, SUSAN, WHAT ARE THE ELVES GOING TO DO?
PLEASE, BROWN OWL, WE'D LIKE TO KEEP IT A SECRET UNTIL THE DAY.
DO TELL US WHAT THE ELVES ARE GOING TO DO, SUSAN.
NO, WE WON'T TELL YOU TILL THE DAY OF THE CHRISTMAS FETE
THE DAY OF THE FETE CAME...
16
WHY, IT'S A MODEL WELL! WHAT ARE YOU GOING TO DO WITH IT, SUSAN - SELL IT?
IT'S ACTUALLY A MODEL OF THE OLD WELL FROM WHICH WE RESCUED A KITTEN.
THE ELVES' WELL WAS A GREAT SUCCESS
17
THERE'S A LONG QUEUE WAITING FOR A DIP, SUSAN. IT WAS A WONDERFUL IDEA OF YOURS.
YES, IT WAS, AND I'M SO PLEASED.
Elves WISHING WELL 6p A Dip
ROLL UP! SIXPENCE A DIP IN THE WISHING WELL!
18
CASH
OUR SECOND PACK VENTURE HAS BEEN A GREAT SUCCESS, BROWNIES. WE HAVE SO MUCH MONEY TO GIVE TO THE CHILDREN'S HOME THAT I SHALL WANT YOU ALL TO HELP ME COUNT IT. THE SIX THAT EARNED THE MOST ARE THE ELVES WITH THEIR WONDERFUL WISHING WELL. WELL DONE, ALL OF YOU, AND ESPECIALLY WELL DONE, THE ELVES!
THE END

CHRISTMAS SONG

Come, says Brown Owl, let us make
Holiday puddings, pies and cake.
Raisins, currants and almond paste,
Icing sugar, now have a taste;
Stir the pudding, find the pot
To boil it up, yes, that's the lot;
Mix the pastry for mincepies
And roll it out to the right size;
Spoon the mincemeat in each pie;

by *Joyce Chapman*

Put them in and let them lie,
Until they turn a golden brown;
Dredge with sugar and cool them down;
Decorate the cake when ready;
Icing takes a hand that's steady;
Now Christmas really has begun;
Getting ready is half the fun.

See if you can find a Christmas pudding in these verses

FUN AND GAMES on LECKHAMPTON HILL

The Devil's Chimney

Three Brownies Enjoy a Day Out with the Editor, Six Cub Scouts and a Kite

Photos by Harry Hammond

On the back of the scarves of the 24th Cheltenham (Leckhampton) Cub Scout Pack is a picture of the Devil's Chimney. This is a famous and very striking landmark in the form of a rocky pinnacle or chimney sticking out from the face of the cliff of Leckhampton Hill. So I arranged to go up Leckhampton Hill with half a dozen Cub Scouts from the Pack for a day of exploration, adventure, photography and kite-flying. I invited three Brownies from the 15th Cheltenham (St. Peter's, Leckhampton) Pack to join us. The Brownies were Sally Goldring, Jane Sylvester and Julia Poyner. I bought the kite, but I didn't have a chance to fly it, as the Cubs and Brownies took it over!

Accompanied by the Group Scout Leader, Mr. J. B. Stringer, and our tame cameraman, away we went. And what a day we had! Brownies aren't exactly sedate, but these Cub Scouts rushed over Leckhampton Hill like a horde of wild Indians!

"It's all right," I told the anxious cameraman. "Let 'em let off steam; then they'll settle down and be nice and quiet when we're ready to take a picture of them for the front cover of the *Sixer Annual.*"

Did I use words like "settle down" and "nice and quiet"? Those young tearaways couldn't be quiet if they were clamped in steel vices! I subdued them for a minute, though, when we reached the Devil's Chimney (which you can see in the photograph at the top of this page). I told them how, when I was a boy and lived in Cheltenham, I had a very daring friend who actually climbed up the Devil's Chimney and

"Can't catch us!"

stood on his head on top. They looked askance at me, as if they didn't believe me, but I assured them that I was telling the truth. That cooled their hot heads. I'm sure none of us would have climbed that formidable chimney of rock, let alone stood on our head on top! The Brownies shuddered at the mere thought of it!

Leckhampton Hill is a marvellous place for exploration, adventure, and fun and games. At the top of a long, steep track, down which a railway once ran, carrying stone from the quarry above, is a row of old kilns, set below the steep cliff of the disused quarry. The Cubs and Brownies had an exciting time climbing up these, peering through the glassless windows (and, of course, clambering through them), walking along the tops and jumping from one to another. In between these activities, they were prevailed upon to pause now and again to allow photographs to be taken. I thought it better to take photographs before they tore their uniforms to shreds, made their hands and faces filthy, or, finally, broke their necks.

Uphill all the way to the old quarry

Hide-and-seek in the old kilns

It's a funny thing, but whenever boys and girls organise games or an outing, sooner or later they'll be joined by a dog. Animals love to play. I remember when I used to play trains on the floor with my small son our cat would hurry in from where-ever he was to join in and pat the train with his paw as it ran along the rails. Who the dog is nobody knows. He's the uninvited guest. He tagged along with us, and had no objection at all to being included in a photograph. In the end he disappeared as suddenly as he came.

I'd bought a fine kite, and it flew splendidly when it wasn't faced with the full force of the wind. Sally especially loved flying it. You can see her in one of the photographs racing off with it as Jane throws it up and Julia keeps the tail from tangling.

On our explorations over the hill we saw a strange thing—a row of three heads rolling about in the grass—at least, that's what it looked like. When we drew closer, we found that the heads belonged to students who were digging in a deep hole for prehistoric remains on the site of a very ancient British camp. This prehistoric camp, of course, was nothing like a modern

Julia, Jane and Sally look out of the window

The Cubs lend a hand

Guide or Scout camp! It was a fortified encampment sited on a hill that was hard for an enemy to reach to attack. After climbing up Leckhampton Hill, I should think an enemy would feel more like taking a nap on the top than launching an assault on a fortified encampment—unless, of course, the enemy were Cub Scouts, who are tireless!

"Are you ready for lunch?" I asked the Cubs and Brownies, and was nearly hurled over the cliff in the rush.

We returned to the cars and drove down to Cheltenham, where our chosen restaurant thought the early Britons really had given up their attack on Leckhampton Hill and launched one on the town! Vast quantities of fish and chips and gallons of fizzy drinks soon disappeared down parched throats into hungry tummies,

Kings of the castle – and queens!

The uninvited guest gets a warm welcome

and for the first time that day a beautiful silence descended. The Editor thought he'd been transported to heaven. Then the bill arrived, and he changed his mind.

The Editor lighter in pocket and the Cubs and Brownies heavier in weight (Sally, who isn't very big, put away an enormous steak), we all sped back to the hill for more fun and games, which included piggy-back races with the Brownies as "jockeys" and investigations into shallow caves in another, huge disused quarry below another part of the hill.

Prior to calling an end to the day, the Editor won sudden popularity by producing from the boot of his car a

Up she goes!

Two of the mysterious rolling heads

Cub horses and Brownie jockeys

Cavemen

No sound but gurgles

"Home, James!" The Brownies wave farewell to Leckhampton Hill as the Editor drives them home

quantity of biscuits and a dozen bottles of a favourite soft drink so gassy that after sipping it the Editor sneezed four times without a pause. You can see the hardened Cub and Brownie drinkers, complete with bottles and straws, happily consuming this deadly brew while the Editor stays out of the picture gasping for air.

This final picnic concluded our outing, so we took the Brownies to their doors and the Cubs back to their long-suffering mothers in the faint hope that the day might have worn them down enough to keep them quiet while poor fathers had their evening meal.

—R.M.

JUNGLE CALLS

by Rikki Taylor

To gain her Discoverer Badge, young Sue
Thought she had better go to the Zoo.
On reaching the place she was quite amazed,
Became quite troubled and almost dazed.
The signposts had gone, and all was noise.
The SEA LIONS were shouting like eager boys.
Sue couldn't see DOVES, but she heard their sound,
ELEPHANTS' noises were all around.
She hurried away to the MONKEYS' home,
And saw where LIONS and TIGERS roam.
The WOLVES gave a call that she could tell.
She heard the PIGS grunting in their dell.
She listened hard and heard the SNAKES,
And the funny noise that the big BEAR makes.
Brownie Sue found her way round the Zoo
By listening to animals—and won the badge too.

Can you sort out the jumbled noises that Sue heard, and say to which animals they belong?

The Wise Owl Says

Sometimes we best show our command of language by saying nothing.

Sympathy is never wasted—except when you give it to yourself.

A tale told about another girl is as hard to unspread as butter.

Religion is like a bank. The more you put in it the more you have to draw upon.

To do nothing is sometimes to do wrong.

Being in a good frame of mind helps to keep you the picture of health.

The shortest way of doing many things is to do one thing at once.

You are growing up when you stop asking where you came from and start asking where you are going.

A religion that costs you nothing is worth exactly what it costs.

Answers to Puzzles

WHICH PATROL FLOWERS?
P. 15: Daffodil; p.82: Primrose

JUNGLE CALLS (p. 81)
Chattering of monkeys; trumpeting of elephants; barks of sea-lions; roars of lions; grunts of pigs; howls of wolves; snarls of tigers; coos of doves; hissing of snakes; growls of bears

WORD WITCHERY (p. 91)
SCOUT, SHOUT, SHOOT, SHOCK, STOCK, STICK, SLICK, SLICE, SLIDE, GLIDE, GUIDE

BROWNIE HOUSE CROSSWORD (p. 61) Solution on page 106

UNION FLAG PUZZLE (p. 64)
1. England. 2. Andrew. 3. Scotland.
4. Patrick. 5. George.

Plays by Brownies (pp. 50–55)
"The Giant and the Gnome" won the prize. The judge thought it had the best plot.

Materials needed: Cardboard plant-pot, paper, newspaper, sticky shapes, twigs, paints, glue.

Tear your white paper into small pieces. Cover your plant-pot with glue; then stick the white pieces of paper all over the plant-pot. Remember to glue also the top of the inside of the plant-pot and cover with the paper.

MAKE YOURSELF A POT OF FLOWERS

M.I. ECKHARDT SHOWS YOU HOW

Screw up your piece of newspaper and place in the bottom of the plant-pot. Draw a circle on your white paper to fit on top of the newspaper.

Now paint your plant-pot a gay colour. Paint your circle brown, then place it on top of the newspaper. This is the soil.

Draw several flower-heads and cut them out. Stick them at the top of your twigs, then push these carefully through your brown circle into the plant-pot.

To complete your pot of flowers, take the sticky shapes and decorate the plant-pot.

Which Guide Patrol Flower?

Copy the outline into each blank frame with the same number and you will discover the name of it

MAKE THIS MODEL FURNITURE

FOR PART OF THE TOYMAKER BADGE (SECTION 3)

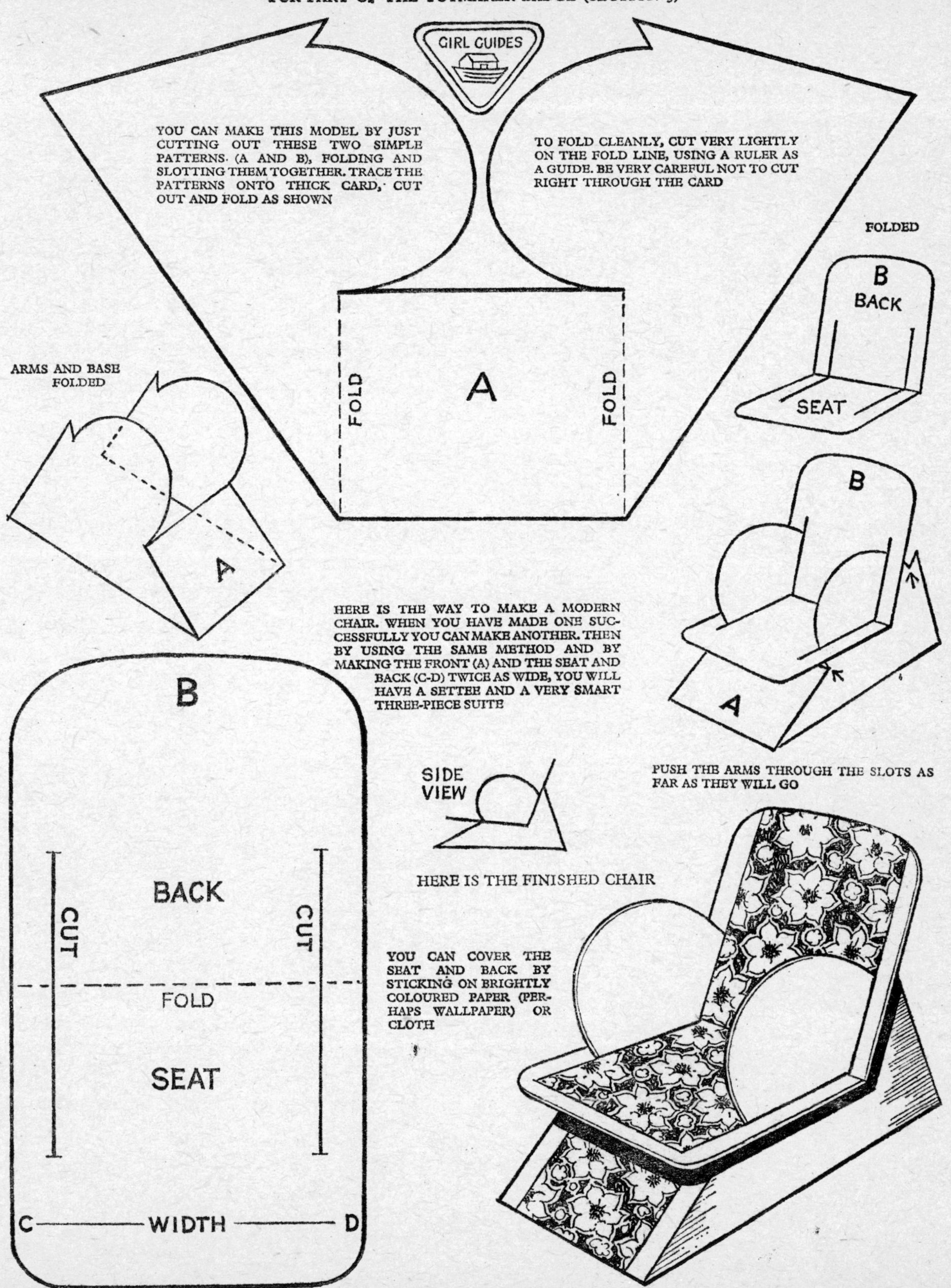

YOU CAN MAKE THIS MODEL BY JUST CUTTING OUT THESE TWO SIMPLE PATTERNS (A AND B), FOLDING AND SLOTTING THEM TOGETHER. TRACE THE PATTERNS ONTO THICK CARD, CUT OUT AND FOLD AS SHOWN

TO FOLD CLEANLY, CUT VERY LIGHTLY ON THE FOLD LINE, USING A RULER AS A GUIDE. BE VERY CAREFUL NOT TO CUT RIGHT THROUGH THE CARD

HERE IS THE WAY TO MAKE A MODERN CHAIR. WHEN YOU HAVE MADE ONE SUCCESSFULLY YOU CAN MAKE ANOTHER. THEN BY USING THE SAME METHOD AND BY MAKING THE FRONT (A) AND THE SEAT AND BACK (C-D) TWICE AS WIDE, YOU WILL HAVE A SETTEE AND A VERY SMART THREE-PIECE SUITE

PUSH THE ARMS THROUGH THE SLOTS AS FAR AS THEY WILL GO

HERE IS THE FINISHED CHAIR

YOU CAN COVER THE SEAT AND BACK BY STICKING ON BRIGHTLY COLOURED PAPER (PERHAPS WALLPAPER) OR CLOTH

THE RIDDLE OF THE . . . .
Thirteenth Page

by
Sydney J. Bounds

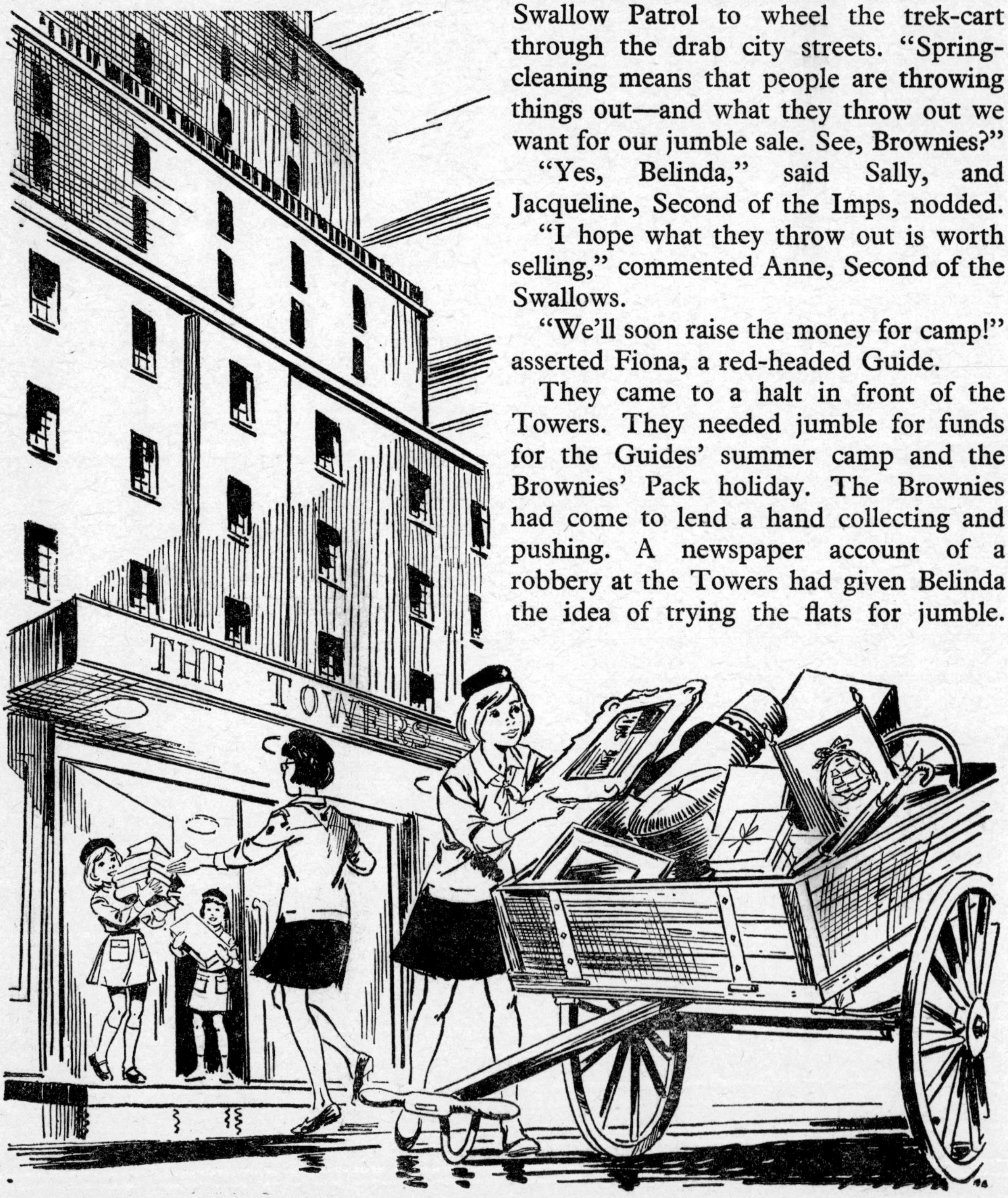

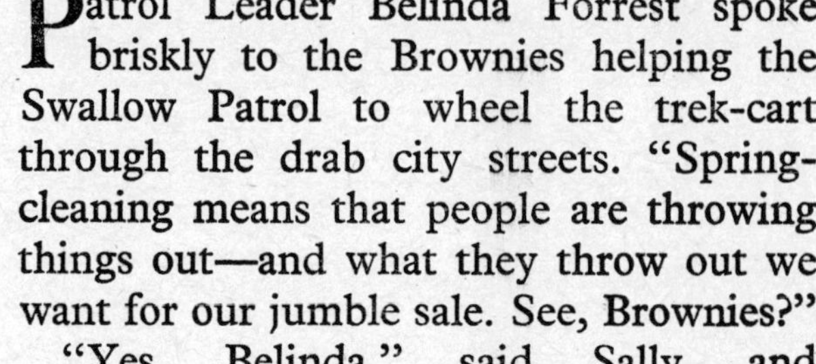

Patrol Leader Belinda Forrest spoke briskly to the Brownies helping the Swallow Patrol to wheel the trek-cart through the drab city streets. "Spring-cleaning means that people are throwing things out—and what they throw out we want for our jumble sale. See, Brownies?"

"Yes, Belinda," said Sally, and Jacqueline, Second of the Imps, nodded.

"I hope what they throw out is worth selling," commented Anne, Second of the Swallows.

"We'll soon raise the money for camp!" asserted Fiona, a red-headed Guide.

They came to a halt in front of the Towers. They needed jumble for funds for the Guides' summer camp and the Brownies' Pack holiday. The Brownies had come to lend a hand collecting and pushing. A newspaper account of a robbery at the Towers had given Belinda the idea of trying the flats for jumble.

"There's bound to be plenty of throw-outs where there is wealth," she told the Brownies.

They all trooped up the steps and into the foyer. The doorman was expecting them. He smiled and said: "Take the lift to the top floor, girls, and work down—you'll find it easier."

They split up and began ringing flat doorbells. For the next half-hour Guides and Brownies were very busy collecting jumble and taking it down in the lift to the trek-cart.

On the sixth floor, as they worked their way down, Belinda noticed a tall, thin, bespectacled Guide reading a paperback from a large pile of books she had just collected.

"That's the Patrol bookworm," she told the Brownies. "Come on, Selina, you slacker," she called to the lanky Guide. "We've a lot to get through this evening. We need all hands to the jumble."

She told the Brownies that Selina always seemed to have her head buried in books. She was an addict of spies and espionage.

"I've read it before, anyway," said Selina regretfully.

Fiona ran up, tripped and knocked the pile of books flying. As she stooped to pick them up, she spotted something.

"An old *Girl Guide Annual*! Can I have this one, Belinda? It's one I haven't got."

"Sorry, Fiona! We need everything for the sale. Camp comes first."

"I'll just hope no one'll buy it!"

The trek-cart groaned under a heavy load as the Guides and Brownies pressed on to the old church hall to get ready for the sale on the Saturday morning.

"Well," Belinda commented later with satisfaction as she looked round the stalls, "we've got plenty of jumble. All we need now is customers!"

"I was told you took away an old *Girl Guide Annual*"

Saturday came. By ten o'clock the drizzle had turned into a heavy downpour. Customers stayed at home.

Belinda turned her gaze from the rain-lashed windows to stalls of books and clothing and household utensils, each priced and manned by Guides and Brownies eager to take money. Only five or six people had turned up so far.

"Total so far, twenty-seven pence in the new decimal currency," said Belinda gloomily. "Not much chance of raising more in this weather. Anybody got any ideas?"

Nobody had. The Swallows looked as gloomy as the weather, except Selina, who was immersed in a spy book. She was so absorbed that she hardly noticed a man come in through the door, hat dripping, rain trickling down his mack on to his trouser bottoms. The man made straight for the bookstall.

"I was told at the Towers that you took away an old *Girl Guide Annual*."

Belinda remembered. So did Jackie and Sally, the Brownies, who came up at that moment. "That's right, sir; we did."

"I'd like to buy it. My daughter, who is a Guide, has a complete set from the first date of publication, except for this particular one. I'll gladly give you a pound for it."

"A pound?" Belinda echoed, and Sally and Jackie looked up with new interest.

The man dipped into his pocket and held out a pound note. "Shall we call it a deal?"

Belinda looked questioningly at Selina. "That *Girl Guide Annual*—where is it?"

"Oh, I let Fiona Burke have it for five new pence. It didn't look as if anyone was coming, and she was keen on it. Like this gentleman, she's got a complete set, but this particular annual was in short supply soon after it came out, I believe Fiona said. She took it home."

"Can you give me the girl's address?" asked the customer. "She might sell it to me. My name is Henson."

Belinda hesitated, but Selina blundered in. "It's fourteen Thirlstone Street." She grinned. "I dare say Fiona will sell it for a pound."

"If she does," said Belinda, "I'll see she pays half back into the camp funds!"

Mr. Henson nodded to them and left. He had not long closed the door, however, when a burly man in a belted raincoat came striding in. Seeing Belinda and Selina by the books, he walked across to them.

"Mr. Henson came in here just now," he said abruptly. "Did he buy anything?"

Belinda stared at him in surprise. "He wanted to buy an old *Girl Guide Annual*."

"Did he get it?" The burly man's angular face looked grim.

"No, we sold it earlier. One of our Guides took it home with her."

"I'd like the address of this Guide. Could you give it to me?"

Belinda looked round, but the Assistant Guider, who had promised to be at the jumble sale, hadn't arrived. Belinda was puzzled. She supposed there was no harm in the second man having Fiona's address, seeing that Selina had given it to Mr. Henson. Rather doubtfully, she gave it.

Selina's eyes gleamed behind her spectacles as the second man hurried out. "There must be a secret document hidden in that *Girl Guide Annual*!" she said.

This time, Belinda was not inclined to snort. She looked serious as she spoke. "I think we ought to check up, having given two men Fiona's address. Fiona told me she had to stay in and look after her small

Fiona gasped. "Is there a secret document in it?"

brother for most of the morning, so she'll be in."

"I'll come with you if you're going to Fiona's," said Selina.

"May we come too?" begged Sally.

"Oh, yes—do let us!" urged Jackie.

Belinda nodded. "I don't see why not," she said.

They met Tammy, the Assistant Guider, in the doorway, and hurriedly explained where they were going.

"I'll come with you," said Tammy briefly. "I think it was unwise to

give Fiona's address to the men. Unfortunately, I was late getting here, or I should have advised against it."

The rain had stopped, and the sun was peeping out. Selina knew a short cut to Fiona's house, but, even so, Mr. Henson was there before them. Fiona, who was alone in the house with her small brother, came to the door in reply to his ring. She had been reading the annual and had it in her hand as she opened the door.

"You must be Fiona Burke," said Mr. Henson pleasantly, eyeing the annual. "I've called to ask you to let me have the *Girl Guide Annual* you and the other Girl Guides collected from the Towers. I want it to complete my daughter's set. I'll give you a pound for it."

"Gosh!" gasped Fiona. "Has it got a secret document or something hidden in it?"

"What d'you mean?" snapped Mr. Henson, his expression changing swiftly. Then he recovered himself. "Ha, ha, nothing like that! As I said, I want it to make up my daughter's complete set."

But Fiona was as sharp as a needle. Mr. Henson's change of face had instantly excited her suspicions.

"It's a good offer," she admitted, "but I'll have to ask my Patrol Leader about it. The annual was collected for the jumble sale, you see, and I shouldn't really have it, I suppose, although I paid for it. I'll let you know when I've seen Belinda about it."

"I can't wait! Here, I'll make it two pounds!" Mr. Henson pulled out two pound notes from his wallet. "I'm in a hurry—urgent business, you know——"

"Sorry, sir," said Fiona politely. "I'm sure I ought to see Belinda first. It might be that the place we got it from ought to be told——"

She got no farther. Mr. Henson, evidently realising that he was up against a stubborn type, darted a quick look down the street, then, in a single movement snatched the annual from Fiona's hand and dashed away.

"Hi!" yelled Fiona. "Come back! I'll

call the police! D'you hear? I'll call——"

At that moment, Belinda, Selina, Tammy and the two Brownies turned the corner. They were in time to see what had happened, even if Fiona's yell hadn't alerted them.

"After him!" snapped Belinda, and broke into a run, Selina, Tammy and the Brownies after her. Fiona joined in. A moment later a seventh added himself to the chase. It was the burly man in a belted raincoat.

Through the streets they raced. Mr. Henson tore across a deserted side-street to a rubbish dump, splashing through pools of water, and then came sharply up against a wood fence. He looked swiftly round, saw that the burly man had taken the lead and was gaining on him, and swerved away on a fresh course. The burly man, however, spurted, made a rugby dive, and wrapped his arms round the other's legs. Mr. Henson crashed to the ground.

Belinda followed up and added her weight, as did Selina and Fiona and the Brownies.

"Got him!" chortled Belinda.

With Tammy arriving within seconds, Mr. Henson had no chance of escaping.

Fiona grabbed the annual from Mr. Henson, who had held on to it even when the tackle brought him down.

"Okay, Franklin," said Mr. Henson glumly. "You win."

"Let him go, girls," said the burly man

The burly man made a dive, and Mr. Henson crashed to the ground

Henson had addressed as Franklin.

"Are you sure?" asked Belinda, looking doubtful.

"He's small time. I can pick him up at any moment. I've got what he was after—that book."

"Are you a secret agent, sir?" asked Selina excitedly.

"More likely a detective," put in Tammy.

Mr. Franklin smiled. "Neither. I work for an insurance company. Don't bother—he's of no importance." Mr. Henson had taken advantage of the distraction to make off. Tammy, despite Mr. Franklin's assurance, would have detained him, but Mr. Henson had no intention of being caught again and was already almost out of sight. "May I take a look at that annual of yours?" Franklin said to Fiona, who, however, thrust the annual firmly under her armpit.

"I feel that this is a Company matter," said Tammy. "Let's go back to the Church Hall and talk about it."

Belinda nodded.

"I'm quite agreeable," said Franklin.

On the way back to the Church Hall, Franklin explained his and Henson's interest in the annual.

"It may be a very good annual," he said, smiling at Fiona, who still kept the book firmly under her armpit, "but I want it for another reason. So did Henson. Somewhere in it is a message."

"I knew it!" cried Selina.

"There was a robbery at the Towers some time back. A jewel-thief named Evans broke in and stole some diamonds, which were in a leather case. He was caught as he left the premises, but, strangely, the diamonds weren't on him and have never been found. They were insured by my company, and we had to pay out for their loss; that's why I'm interested in getting them back. Evans went to jail for breaking into the Towers, even though the theft of the jewels couldn't be charged against him. From prison he smuggled a message out to Henson, a copy of which came into the possession of my company. It's pretty certain that the message hides the vital clue to the whereabouts of the diamonds, but all it says is *1959 Girl Guide Annual*."

"So the diamonds may be hidden in this annual I've got!" cried Fiona, and began to turn the pages over with trembling fingers.

"Not the actual diamonds, I think," said Franklin, "but a clue to their whereabouts."

Not until the Church Hall was reached would Fiona let the annual out of her hands.

Methodically then, Franklin turned every page. He found nothing. As he reached the last page, he frowned, and said: "I suppose there could have been a paper inside and it could have fallen out. I don't think so, though, because the reference was to the 1959 *Girl Guide Annual* as if the clue was in the book itself, rather than in something separate from it."

"Please let me have a look through it," begged Selina. "It could be a code."

Eagerly, though slowly, she turned the pages, running her finger carefully down each column.

"Pinpricks—no! Invisible ink—could be, but we'd have to apply . . . ah, what's this?" She had reached page thirteen, and she grew more and more excited as she ran her finger down the page. "There are dots—yes, look—all down the page!"

Crowding round her, Franklin and the Guides followed her pointing finger. They saw what the eager eyes of Selina had so cleverly spotted—a faint dot over one letter on each of a number of lines. Belinda pulled out a ballpoint pen and began to write down each letter as Selina called it out. When they had finished, she read out the completed message:

AIR DUCT SIXTH FLOOR

"So that's it!" breathed Franklin. "That explains how the police missed them too. They never thought of Evans going up a floor. The robbery was on the fifth floor.

Who'd have thought he'd go up a floor when he was running away to the street to get away from the scene of the crime? Come on—we'd better go and collect!"

The Guides and Brownies could hardly wait. Even Tammy was excited. The jumble sale was almost forgotten in the excitement of the moment. There had been so few customers, anyway, as Belinda pointed out, that their presence at the hall could easily be dispensed with, though Tammy reluctantly decided she must stay.

Sally thrust her hand into the ventilator

The girls and Mr. Franklin hurried to the Towers. There, theory was quickly put to the test. Sally was hoisted up to a ventilator set high up in the wall of the corridor on the sixth floor. After tense moments, she thrust her hand in and pulled out a small leather case. When this was opened, the eyes of all the girls were dazzled by a handful of brilliant diamonds set against black velvet.

"I don't wonder about the saying that diamonds are a girl's best friend," murmured Belinda. "Aren't they just fabulous!"

Franklin rubbed his hands. "There's a reward for the recovery of these," he told her, "and I'll see you get it. The reward, I believe I'm right in saying, is fifty pounds."

"Fifty pounds!" cried Belinda. "That'll mean a new annual for Fiona, the latest spy thriller for Selina and summer camp and Pack holiday de luxe for the Blackwich Guides and Brownies."

Mr. Franklin held out his hand in turn to each of them. "It means a lot to me too," he said simply. "Thanks for your help."

As they set off back to the Church Hall, the rain stopped and the sun came out, and when they reached the hall they found it packed with customers.

"Anyway, I'm jolly glad they didn't get here in time to buy the *Girl Guide Annual*," Fiona remarked, with a chuckle. "We wouldn't have made fifty pounds."

WORD WITCHERY

You can't turn a Scout into a Guide—or can you? Be a word witch and change this Scout into a Guide by changing ONE letter at a time. Here are some clues to help you :-

SCOUT

1. To call loudly ....
2. You could do this with a gun ....
3. What the wind did to the trees ....
4. A little accident can give you this ....
5. Could be useful to have in the larder ....
6. A dry one is more useful for lighting a fire ....
7. Quick ....
8. A piece of cake, perhaps ....
9. Best made on a slope; not on the footpath, please ....
10. To move gracefully ....

GUIDE

THE FLOWER DISPLAY

by Grace Lumley

THE 1st Townlea Pack lived in the middle of a big industrial town. Most of the Brownies lived in flats with no gardens, so were rather startled when their Guider suggested that they should all grow something as a Pack Venture.

They all listened quietly as Mrs. Gordon explained how seeds have to be planted and then watered carefully and looked after until they become lovely flowers.

"Please may I help to grow something?" asked Mandy.

"And me too?" squeaked Penny.

"Why, you two haven't even made your Promise yet!" laughed Gillian, Sixer of the Elves.

"Please let me, then!" pleaded Laura, who was eight.

"We will all join in," smiled Mrs. Gordon. "We'll grow seeds in pretty pots. When they're all in flower, we'll ask the District Commissioner to come and look at them. Then we'll each think of an old person who would like a pot of flowers, and take them round."

The Brownies were delighted.

"Shall we bring our pots next week, Brown Owl?"

"What seeds can we grow?"

"My granny loves tulips!"

"Bring pots!" cried Mrs. Gordon. "Wouldn't you like to make your own?"

Everyone looked surprised at this, and rather doubtful.

"It's great fun," the Guider went on. "Now listen carefully. Next week I want each of you to bring an old newspaper, a paint-brush, scissors, and a little 'shaper' of some kind."

"What's a shaper?" murmured Penny to her friend Anthea.

"An old cup with no handle—a little pudding basin—an empty flower-pot—anything that would make a nice shape for a flower-bowl," explained Mrs. Gordon, as if she had overheard Penny. "Please don't bring anything that might break—like a glass tumbler or your mother's best china sugar-bowl! You will need aprons, too."

"I'll bring some old Christmas-cards," said Miss Tess, the Assistant Guider. "We can use the thin white paper in the middle as well as the pictures."

"Whatever for, Tawny?" asked Maisie.

"You'll see!" laughed Miss Tess.

Next week the Brownies all turned up early. They produced a marvellous assortment of "shapers". Maisie had an old cracked plastic cereal bowl. Millie had a pretty cup with two big cracks down one side and no handle. Penny had brought a baby's polythene beaker.

"Baby had a new one for Christmas," Penny explained, "and she doesn't use this one now."

Before they made the Brownie Ring, Miss Tess showed them how to tear their newspapers into small pieces about three inches square and put them into a bowl of water. She did the same with the thin white pieces torn out of Christmas-cards.

The Guider spread two trestle-tables with newspaper. She made wallpaper paste and put it into four big jars.

When the paper was well soaked and ready to use, Miss Tess showed them what to do. "First of all, rub a thin film of Vaseline over the outside of your 'shapers' so that they will slide out easily. Now place a thin layer of wet newspaper over the outside of your shaper, letting it stand upside-down on the table, as you have to do the bottoms as well. Next, take your brush and paste all over the paper. Now add another layer of paper and more paste, and go on like that until you have a thickness of about half an inch. You must press each layer firmly, so that it all sticks well and keeps a nice, even shape. Put a layer of white paper to finish off. Be careful that no newsprint shows."

"I am glad you brought your aprons," said Mrs. Gordon, glancing at Penny, who had pasted more on herself than on her bowl.

Miss Tess laid out the Christmas-cards, and the Brownies picked out which ones they wanted and cut out small pictures of robins, holly-leaves and flower-heads. They had to paste the pictures round the outsides of the bowls. Although Mrs. Gordon had explained carefully that they must put their bowls up the right way before sticking on pictures, Penny kept her "shaper" upside-down, so

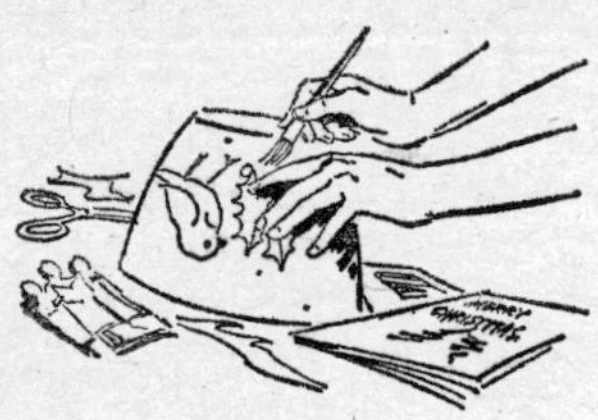

that all her pictures of "angels" ended up standing on their heads!

When Miss Tess pointed out her mistake, Penny said, "I like them best with their feet in the air and their heads in their saucers!"

The Brownies had to leave their pots all the week to dry out. At the next Pack meeting they "eased out" the "shapers" and varnished the pots inside and out to make them waterproof and shiny.

The following week they planted their seeds. They had two kinds of seeds. Miss Tess had brought two bags of soil. The Brownies who chose nasturtiums used gritty sand. Those who chose virginia stock used bulb fibre. Miss Tess said these seeds needed richer, moister soil and that they would grow all over the surface like a fairies' carpet of lovely mixed colours.

All the Brownies looked after their bowls with great care. It did seem a long time, though, before the seeds produced flowers.

At last the day came when the Brownies were able to give their flower display. Many parents came on the day, and so did the District Commissioner, who said she could not judge which was the best because they were all so lovely.

She laughed at Penny's "angels" doing handstands round her bowl!

"What a good thing it is that your flowers haven't grown upside-down!" she said.

Afterwards, the Brownies went out and delivered their gifts to old people, who were delighted with them.

The Townlea Pack decided after this to have a display every year. They agreed to make it an annual Pack Venture, but to grow *three* bowlfuls of flowers each!

THE DISCOVERER BADGE

Here are some pictures to help you gain the Discoverer Badge. They show the names and appearance of living creatures, trees and flowers that you will need to know. Find the real ones yourself, or spot them in the woods and meadows. Then discover something interesting and distinctive about them

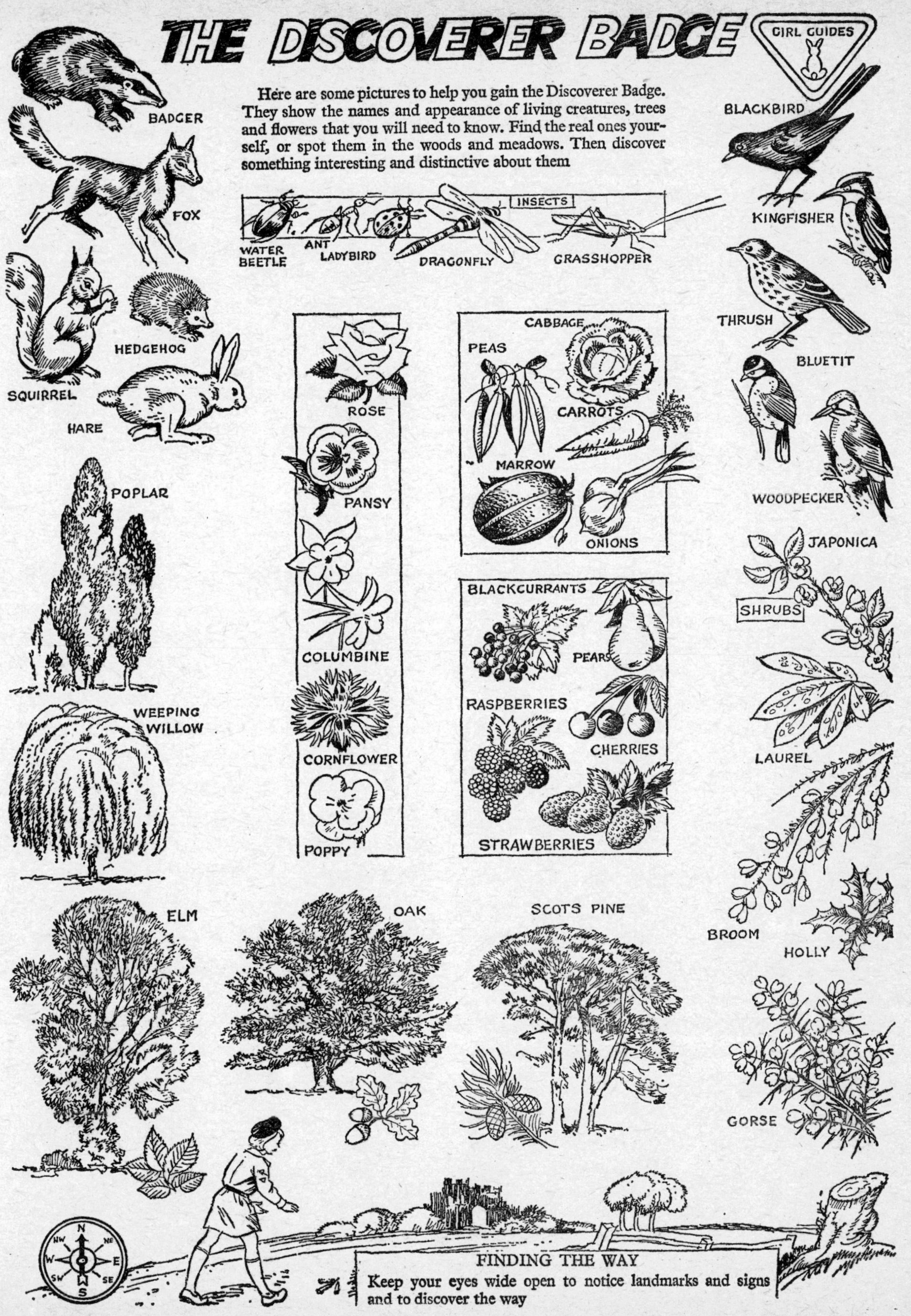

FINDING THE WAY

Keep your eyes wide open to notice landmarks and signs and to discover the way

God Save the Queen!

Jane Willis Tells You Interesting Facts about the National Anthem

One of the Challenges given in the *Brownie Guide Handbook* on the Brownie Highway is to "know and understand the first and last verses of the National Anthem".

The tune of the National Anthem is one that everyone knows; in fact, it's been "top of the pops" for more than two hundred years. It all began with Bonnie Prince Charlie! It was in July, 1745, that he landed in Scotland, raised an army and set off to invade England. King George II, however, defeated him at Culloden, which you may have learned about, and forever ended the hopes of the Jacobites, who wanted to restore Bonnie Prince Charlie to the throne.

During these troubled times a patriotic hymn was sung at Drury Lane Theatre, London, entitled "God Save our Lord the King". It was also published in the *Gentleman's Magazine* as a song for two voices, but no one really knew who wrote the tune or the words, and they still don't to this day! It was sung by Henry Carey, who composed "Sally in Our Alley", and he claimed to be the author of the words and composer of the music; but it is thought he only arranged and adapted a version that was written by Dr. John Bull, who was organist and composer to Queen Elizabeth and King James I.

A feeling of national pride was sweeping across the country, and "God Save the King" was adopted as the National Anthem. From that time it has been used on all state and royal occasions.

Just as most countries have an emblem to fly—their flag—so too they have a national song. Most of these anthems proclaim devotion to a king or queen, but during the French Revolution, after the French king had lost his throne, national anthems changed and were sung in praise of freedom and the people of republics that had neither king nor queen. The French national anthem is called *La Marsellaise*. That of America is *The Star Spangled Banner*.

Many famous composers have used the tune of God Save the Queen in their work, Haydn, Brahms and Beethoven among them.

One verse that you do not have to learn was in the original song. Perhaps it's just as well! Here it is:

Scatter his enemies and make
them fall;
Confound their politics,
Frustrate their knavish tricks;
On him our hopes are fixed;
O save us all.

GIFT-MAKES FOR BROWNIE GUIDES

by Molly Walmsley

DOOR DECORATIONS FOR CHRISTMAS

Most garments nowadays are returned from cleaners on a thin wire coat-hanger. These are ideal for use as door decorations, or for hanging on walls or picture-rails.

With strong thread, bind evergreens attractively on the hanger. Some of the foliage can be touched with silver lacquer or glue and glitter to give a frosted effect.

When dry, tie one large coloured bauble so that it hangs from the centre on a thread, or three baubles on threads of different lengths. Tie a bow of red ribbon near the hook to finish off.

In the same way, door decorations can also be made from a circle of strong wire—perhaps saved from an old lampshade.

The smallest size red baubles look very effective tied at intervals among the green foliage.

MAKE A BLOTTER

A blotter makes quite a useful Christmas present.

Cut a piece of stiff cardboard about 12″ x 16″ and two pieces each 12″ x 3″. Cover each piece with leftover wallpaper, glueing firmly at back.

Place wrong side of small pieces to each end of large piece on right side, and secure the three outer edges with sticky tape.

Slip several sheets of blotting paper cut to size into the holder, and it is ready for use.

A longer lasting one can be made by using "contact" or a similar covering, which can be wiped clean when necessary.

A CHRISTMAS PLANT POT

Fill a plant pot (about the 6″ size) with sand or soil, packing it firmly. From the hedgerow, choose a branchy twig about 15″–18″ high, and "plant" it firmly in the pot.

Paint the branch with shoe whitener or silver lacquer. When dry, tie gaily wrapped sweets to the branches. Over the soil put a circle of polythene, covering this with cottonwool to represent snow and arranging a layer of sweets on it. To finish off, fix a silver star to the topmost branch, or a tiny doll dressed as an angel or fairy.

The plant pot could be painted or covered with red or green crepe paper if desired.

As a Christmas good turn, you could make several of these to give away.

START A COIN COLLECTION

Suggests John Willis

Yes, coins, not cones! Like stamps, coins are not only interesting to collect, but can be profitable too. Only a very small outlay is needed to start a collection. In fact, you can start by looking through your pennies and halfpennies for rare dates. Halfpennies are no longer in use, but there are still some about.

You cannot collect every sort of coin for every reign—at least, not until you have a lot more time and money than you are likely to have at the moment! So begin by deciding which type of coin attracts you the most. Gold and silver coins are too costly, so you must begin with the humble old penny.

Take a look at an old penny that is in good condition and you will see that there's more to it than a piece of old copper!

Start your collection by buying, or borrowing from a public library, a book that will tell you of the rarer dates of issue. Try to find coins in good condition and keep those of different dates. You will be able to replace worn coins with better ones as time goes by. You may be lucky enough to find a very rare penny—a 1951, for instance. There were only 120,000 issued in that year, and most of those went to the Bahamas, so it is a valuable and much-sought-after penny.

As your collection grows you will enjoy looking out for rare coins. You may find it worth while to pester grandmothers, uncles and other relatives to see what they may have tucked away in jewel-boxes or bureau drawers.

Keeping your coins in good condition once you have found them becomes a problem as your collection grows bigger. They must be kept in a warm, dry place, but it's wise not to leave them where people in the house can easily get at them, or you may find your precious Victorian penny in your brother's dinner money or that a special shilling has been put into the gas meter by mistake!

You can buy folders to put your

coins in, but it's quite possible to make one that is suitable.

Take a sheet of stiff white card and get a grown-up to draw round the coins with a fine point to get the exact size and shape. Then ask your helper to get a sharp razor-blade and cut carefully just inside the drawn circle. Stick this on to another plain sheet of card, which forms a backing, then push your coins into place. If they don't stay firmly in place use a tiny piece of plasticine on the back of the coin. Place the coins in order of years and neatly print the date underneath. Stored like this they do not rub against each other and are very pleasing to look at.

Here are a few dates to look for until you get your own booklet:-

Pennies

1932 1934 1950 1951 1953

Halfpennies

1913 1925 1946 1953

The Editor Nearly Grows Rich. Having made a practice for years of putting aside halfpennies rather than loading his pockets with them and pulling them out in mistake for shillings, the Editor read this article on collecting coins with keen interest.

He rushed to his store of ha'pennies. Almost the first one he picked up was dated 1913—a rare year! He asked an expert on coins how much it was worth.

"If it is in good condition," was the reply, "eighteen pence—eighteen new pence, that is."

Well, this only goes to show, doesn't it, that you might be richer than you thought! Hurry up! You might have a rare coin among your old pennies and halfpennies, if you've kept some!

Barbara was puzzled. She had been hurrying home from Brownies when she spotted a brown beret lying on the pavement.

"I wonder who it can belong to?" she thought. She looked inside for a name-tag. Sure enough, there was a name inside. "Christine Donovan," murmured Barbara.

Barbara saw a brown beret lying on the pavement

The Mystery

"We have no Christine Donovan in our Pack. I wonder who she can be."

Barbara lived in quite a small town, so she knew most of the Brownies who lived there.

"Perhaps she is in the other Pack," she thought. "I'll ask Mummy to ring up the Brown Owl when I get home."

"Doesn't it belong to one of your own Brownies?" asked Mrs. Bremner, when Barbara reached home and showed her the beret she'd found.

"No, we have no Christine Donovan in our Pack," Barbara told her.

Her mother phoned the Brownie Guider who ran the second Pack in Callinford.

"Mrs. Carson, the Brown Owl, has no one of the name of Christine Donovan in her Pack," she reported after her phone conversation.

"This is a real mystery," said Barbara. "I can hardly wait to tell Jennifer about it." Jennifer was Barbara's best friend.

Next morning was Saturday, and Barbara and Jennifer were going shopping for their mothers. Barbara told Jennifer about the beret.

"It is peculiar, isn't it?" said Jennifer. "I wonder who Christine Donovan can be?"

"What do you think we should do, Jen?"

"We could look in the telephone directory as soon as we get home," Jennifer suggested. "We might find a Donovan in there."

As soon as shopping was finished, the girls hurried home to look in the telephone directory.

"Donaghue . . . Donohoe . . . Donon . . . Don's Dry Cleaners. . . ." Barbara's finger went down the list of names. "Jen, there are no Donovans in the whole book!"

of the Lost Beret

by Marian Rhodes

"Are you sure? Well, what do we do now?"

"Maybe we should just give up," said Barbara.

"You know, we could take the beret to Brownies next week," Jennifer said. "Perhaps Brown Owl will suggest something."

Next Friday evening the Brownies had a special Thinking Day meeting. Pictures of Brownies in the uniform of different countries were posted around the room. The Brownies sat in a circle for Pow-wow.

"Well, now, Brownies," said Mrs. Tait, "can anyone tell me something about Brownies in another country?"

"Please, Brown Owl," Mary, the Sprites Sixer said, "the Brownies in the Cook Islands, off New Zealand, make their own hats out of coconut palms. The people who live there are called Maoris."

"Very good, Mary. Wouldn't it be fun to make part of your own uniform!"

"Brown Owl," Barbara said, "I found a beret on the pavement on my way home from Brownies last week, and I can't find out who it belongs to."

"Is there a name inside?" asked Mrs. Tait.

"Yes, the name is Christine Donovan, but there's no Brownie in this Pack or in the second Callinford named Christine Donovan."

"Pass it round, Barbara, please," said Mrs. Tait. "Let's all examine it."

The brown beret was passed around and examined by all the Brownies, by the Assistant Guider, and by Mrs. Tait.

"There are no Donovans in the telephone directory," volunteered Jennifer.

"I can see you have been using your thinkpieces, anyway," said Mrs. Tait. "Well, how would you like us all to put our heads together on this and make a Pack Venture of finding the owner of the beret? We'll use our eyes, our ears, even our noses if necessary! If you find any clues or have ideas about the beret, bring them to Pack meeting. How about that? You can work in Sixes."

All the Brownies voted the idea excellent.

On their way home from the meeting Barbara and Jennifer talked about the Pack Venture.

"Perhaps we'll find out who the beret does belong to now," said Barbara.

"Barbara, dear, will you check to see if the milkman has been?" Barbara's mother called to her next morning.

Barbara went to the front door, but the empty bottles were still there on the step.

"No, Mummy," she called, and was just about to close the door when she noticed something white sticking out from below one of the bottles. She picked up the paper and opened it, but it was blank.

"What is it, Barbara?" asked Mrs. Bremner, as Barbara came into the kitchen looking puzzled.

"I don't really know," said Barbara. "This piece of paper was under one of the milk bottles, but it's only blank."

Just then there came a knock at the door. It was Jennifer, bright and early. "I thought we might go for a walk or some-

"Look! There's writing beginning to appear!"

thing; it's so lovely and sunny this morning."

"I found this under a milk bottle." Barbara fluttered the paper in front of Jennifer's face.

Jennifer examined the paper on both sides. "It's only a blank piece of paper," she said, sniffing at it.

"What *are* you doing?" asked Barbara.

"Using my nose—remember?" said Jennifer. "There's a smell of vinegar coming from it."

"From your nose?"

"No, silly, from the paper. Here, have a sniff!"

Barbara sniffed it on both sides.

"It seems stronger on the one side," she declared. "The paper seems damp. Let's dry it by the fire."

The two girls sat on the floor in front of the fireplace, and began to dry the paper, holding it well away from the flames.

"*Jen!*" cried Barbara. "Look what's happening!"

"Writing!" breathed Jennifer. "Now I remember! People use vinegar for invisible ink. You have to warm it by the fire to make it visible. The writing's clear now."

"Read it!" cried Barbara.

Jennifer read out:

"BROWN MY INK, AND BROWN MY HAT
TELL ME WHAT YOU THINK OF THAT!
COME TO THE PARK AT THE HOUR OF THREE
AND FOLLOW THE SHADOW TO HELP FIND ME.
P.S. USE YOUR NOSES TO FIND THE ROSES.

C.D.

"And it's signed C.D." Jennifer gazed excitedly at Barbara. "C.D. stands for Christine Donovan! This is really something, Barbara."

"Let's get the Imp Six together this afternoon. We'll tell them about the message."

Jennifer was crossing the street on her way home to lunch when she spied Lucy

Jenkins, one of the Gnomes, hurrying along.

"Hello, Lucy! Where are you off to?" she asked.

"Ha, wouldn't you like to know," said Lucy mysteriously. "We've got a clue to the mystery of the brown beret. I've just been to our Sixer's house. The Gnomes are going to solve the mystery of the beret." She ran off round the corner, leaving Jennifer rather bewildered.

Later that afternoon, when the Imps had met at the entrance to the park, she told them of her meeting with Lucy Jenkins.

"That's strange! One of the girls in the Kelpies acted in much the same way," said Barbara. "We didn't breathe a word about our clue, though. Oh, do get up, Biddy," she said crossly, as Biddy, the plump one of the Imp Six, sat on the park bench and began to eat a chocolate bar.

"Oh, let's *all* sit down for a while," suggested Jennifer. "There's no sense in getting bad-tempered over this."

They all sat in a row along a park bench, and tried to think what the rhyme meant.

"Are you sure it said a shadow?" asked Biddy, her mouth full of chocolate.

"Yes, positive," said Barbara.

"What kind of a shadow?" asked Lesley, the youngest Brownie.

"Perhaps it's the shadow of a beret," laughed Jessie.

"Come on, let's use our noses, to find the roses, as the message says," suggested Jennifer.

The Six wandered off through the bushes. The park was really just a piece of waste ground where children played, but recently it had been improved, and gardens and fishponds had been added.

Lesley was the first to find the rose garden. It was in another part of the park and entered through a small door in a stone wall. The scent of the roses was very strong.

"Oh, this is beautiful!" exclaimed Jennifer.

There were roses climbing over archways; others grew in rose-beds.

"Well, what do we do now that we've found the roses?" asked Biddy.

"Come here!" Jennifer's excited voice reached them from behind an archway covered in red rambling roses. She was standing by a sundial, looking very excited. "Are you wearing your watch, Barbara?"

"Yes, why?"

"Is it three o'clock yet?"

"Yes, it's right on the stroke of three."

Just then, as though in agreement, the church clock struck three.

"Well, come and see the shadow. I'll bet this is what the message means." Jennifer pointed to the finger, which cast a shadow across the face of the sundial.

The Brownies studied the shadow very carefully, then walked in the direction in which it pointed. Lesley was the one to find something. She gave a loud whoop,

and held up an envelope. She was jumping up and down excitedly.

"What is it?"

"Where was it?"

"It was attached on a rose-bush, right opposite the sundial." Lesley held up the envelope and shook it. "It rattles," she said, handing it to Barbara.

They all sat down around the base of the sundial, as Barbara tipped the contents of the envelope into her lap.

There was an old bus ticket, a Guide Patrol emblem, a roughly drawn map, and another verse:

PUT THEM TOGETHER AND
WHAT HAVE YOU GOT?
A BUS TRIP TO A LOVELY SPOT
IF MUM SAYS YES, WE'LL SEE
YOU THERE,
SO "BE PREPARED" A SURPRISE
TO SHARE!

"Put them together?" queried Jessie. "Put what together?"

Barbara studied the map, and noticed a drawing of a flower on one part of it. Jennifer was looking at the Guide emblem.

"What do you suppose this is?" she asked. "Looks like a marguerite, or a daisy or something."

"Let me see it," said Barbara. She examined the emblem, and then the little drawing in the map. They were very much alike.

"I'd say it was a daisy," said Lesley.

"That's it! That is it!" Barbara was staring at the three items from the envelope. "Do you remember the new Guide campsite that opened last month, Jen?"

"Hello, there! cried the Guide, and waved

"Oh, yes! What was its name—Primrose Dell or something?"

"No! Listen! It was *Daisy Grove*, and I think this message means we have to take a bus trip out to the Guide camp. I'll bet that is where we'll solve the mystery of Christine Donovan."

"Do you really think so?" Jennifer was rather doubtful.

"Tomorrow is Sunday. Do you think your parents will let you come?" Barbara looked round at the Six.

"Well, we can only ask," said Biddy.

"We'll leave it at that, then," said Barbara. "If you can't come you can phone to let me know. If I don't hear from you, we shall meet at the bus stop at one o'clock."

There was great excitement that night. Mrs. Bremner agreed to have Jennifer again for the night, and seemed quite willing for them to take the bus ride to the Guide camp. Unfortunately, all the other members of the Six had to stay at home.

"Isn't this fun, Jen?" said Barbara, as they settled in the bus. "I'm surprised that Mummy has been so understanding about it."

"I know! I was thinking the same thing," said Jennifer. "Mine usually won't let me go on bus trips without her."

Daisy Grove was only about ten miles away from the town in which the girls lived, so it was not too long a journey, and it seemed to pass very quickly. They got out at a village and asked directions to the Guide camp.

"Look, here comes a Guide!" said Barbara, and pointed to a girl in blue running towards them.

"Hello, there!" the Guide called and waved.

Barbara and Jennifer ran to meet her. "Are you from the Daisy Grove Guide camp?" they asked.

"Yes. I came to see if we were having any visitors."

"Well, I suppose you could call us that," said Barbara. "We received a message that told us to come here—at least, we think that's what it meant."

"What are your names?" the Guide asked.

"I'm Barbara and this is Jennifer, my Second."

"Well, I am Midge—Marjory, really, but I got the name Midge at camp."

They followed Midge through a gate which led to a path by the side of a field. After what seemed a long trudge they saw a "horseshoe" of white tents, which meant they had reached Daisy Grove.

Midge was just about to leave them for a moment when Jennifer blurted out, "Do you know Christine Donovan?"

A curious expression came on Midge's face. Suddenly she began to laugh. Then she excused herself and hurried away.

"Well, I must say that was very rude of her," said Jennifer.

A moment later they were greeted by a Guider, who appeared from behind a large barn.

"Hello, Barbara and Jennifer!"

Barbara and Jennifer almost dropped to the ground in amazement.

"Brown Owl!"

"Brown Owl—well! You're here too!"

"Whatever did you say to make Midge react the way she did?" asked Mrs. Tait.

"I asked her if she knew Christine Donovan," said Jennifer. "She laughed her head off."

"I don't wonder. You girls have been very clever, and I think it's time that we let you into the mystery."

"Why are you here, Brown Owl?" Barbara asked curiously.

"The Guide Guider happens to be my sister. She needed some help in running the camp. It is a new site, so there is a lot of work to do. I volunteered to help. Now, there is someone I think you would like to meet—Christine Donovan."

"Christine Donovan!" cried both Brownies together.

"Do you mean it?" asked Barbara eagerly.

Mrs. Tait nodded. "Come with me."

Excitedly, they followed Brown Owl into the barn, which was a storage place for tents and other equipment.

"Here she is," said Mrs. Tait, and stood aside to let them see a figure in Brownie uniform standing by a toadstool in the corner.

"Why, Brown Owl," cried Barbara, "this is a *doll*."

"She is almost life-size," said Jennifer. "I thought she was a real Brownie."

"She is Christine Donovan," laughed Mrs. Tait, "and you found her beret. It's quite simple, really. Christine Donovan is the Guide Company's mascot. The uniform and the beret belonged to a Brownie called Christine Donovan, and the girls didn't remove the name-tag. Now do you understand? I only learned about it, of course, after you'd found the beret and brought it to Pack meeting. The Guides were on their way to camp, and

BROWNIE HOUSE CROSSWORD (p. 61)

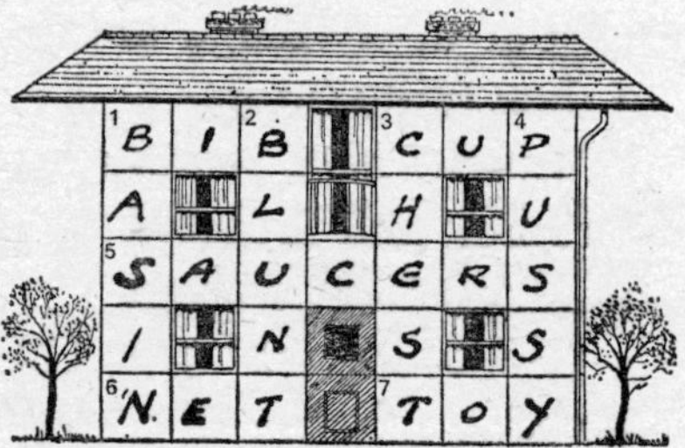

the beret must have come off and was left unnoticed where you found it, Barbara."

"Well!" exclaimed Barbara.

"The mystery is solved at last!" laughed Jennifer.

"When I discovered that Christine

"This is yours," said Midge to the mystified Brownies

Donovan was a Guide Company's doll mascot, I decided to prepare a few clues, messages and things for the Brownie Pack."

"So you were responsible for the verses and things!" said Barbara.

"And the invisible ink," added Jennifer.

"Tawny Owl did most of it, but I was responsible for trying to get some of you here to see a Guide camp."

They went outside into the sunlight, where they met Midge.

"They're all yours, Midge," Mrs. Tait said, and disappeared inside the barn again.

Midge led them to the horseshoe of tents. "This is yours," she said, leading them inside one of the tents.

"What do you mean?" asked Barbara, mystified.

"Tomorrow being a holiday, you have been given permission to stay for a while here at the Guide camp—from before breakfast till after camp-fire—and to have the use of this tent. Your parents were told about it by your Guider, and have agreed."

Barbara and Jennifer were speechless. They were thrilled.

"I still can't take it all in," said Barbara, looking dazed.

"There's just one thing I'd like to say," said Jennifer.

"What's that?"

"Three cheers for Christine Donovan!"

WOLVES at the DOOR

A True Story of a Guide's Hair-Raising Adventure in Canada by Jean Howard

Julie could still hardly believe her good fortune when she was chosen to exchange with a Canadian Guide for the Christmas holidays. Certainly she had worked hard at French at school, and had spent many hours skiing in the Scottish hills, near her home-town of Inverness. These two accomplishments and an excellent report from her Guider had all weighed in her favour, and now here she was, staying with her hostess, Anne MacDonald, in a small township at the foot of the Rocky Mountains.

The two Guides had met in Winnipeg for the big "round-up", and when that was over travelled westwards together. As the rolling prairies gradually gave way to dense forests and deep, silent lakes, the scenery became more and more awe-inspiring. As they neared their destination and saw the snow-capped mountains, Julie could hardly wait to go skiing down the smooth white slopes.

For three days there was sunshine and blue skies, and they had some splendid runs, but then the weather changed. Julie looked out of the window at the snow-flakes swirling past, and turned back thankfully to the blazing log fire.

She was telling Anne and her mother about Inverness and her Guide Company there when Anne's brother Duncan came in. He told them there had been reports of thefts of fur pelts from the trappers' log cabins. Old Pierre Lachasse had complained that many of his best pelts had been stolen; he could ill afford to lose the dollars they would have fetched.

The next morning was fine again. As Julie would soon have to leave, she and Anne decided to go on one more grand expedition.

They climbed upwards for several hours and then stuck their skis in the snow and made a seat with their sticks. They sat and gazed at the wonderful view while enjoying the sandwiches and fruit Anne's mother had packed up for them.

Anne pointed out the route they would ski down. Then they put their skis on again and climbed up farther so that Julie could take some photographs from the shoulder of the mountain where it sloped down to a great forest and the river in the valley below. The view was tremendous, and the girls stood there for some time, finding it difficult to leave such a magnificent scene.

Then quite suddenly Julie found herself shivering. She looked up and saw heavy clouds moving across the sun. Within minutes a white mist began to envelope them.

"Quick!" cried Anne. "Put away your camera. We must start making our way down at once. This is what we call a 'white-out'. I can see we are in for a storm."

Slipping the rucksack on to her back, Anne pulled on her gloves. Gripping her ski-sticks, she glided gracefully downhill. Julie followed close behind, and they ran on for some way. The mist became denser and everything grew white and featureless.

After a while Anne slowed to a standstill. Julie could see she was worried.

"We ought to be nearly down by now, but I don't recognise any of the usual landmarks. We'd better go extra carefully in case we come to a sudden drop."

They continued downwards until they found themselves on the edge of a thick forest, where Anne realised they were completely lost.

"We must have come down the wrong side of the mountain in the mist," she said. "It makes everywhere look the same."

Carrying their skis on their shoulders, they slipped and stumbled down through the tall conifers until they came to a frozen lake.

In a clearing was a tumbledown log cabin. Here at least was shelter. As they pushed open the creaking door and groped their way inside, the storm broke overhead, sending large snowflakes drifting down through the trees, which were already bending their tall masts in the wind.

It was dark and gloomy inside, and the girls agreed that the first thing was to try and light a fire. Julie found a few bits of dry kindling wood in a corner. While she

The girls pushed open the creaking door

A bearded man with a gun burst through the door

searched for the matches in the rucksack, Anne went outside and collected a good supply of dead sticks and branches, which were fairly dry. By much puffing and blowing they eventually coaxed the fire into a cheerful blaze.

The only furniture was a rickety old chair, a stool, and a small wooden bed against the wall. The girls sat down thankfully by the fire and finished the rest of their picnic. Outside it grew steadily darker as the storm raged overhead.

They were sharing the last sandwich when there was a sudden noise outside. The door burst open and a tall, bearded man with a gun staggered into the hut. He stopped abruptly and stared at the two girls.

"Dommage! What do you here?" he cried out in broken English.

"Good evening!" answered Anne, trying not to show her alarm. "I'm afraid we lost our way in the mist and took shelter here. Is this your cabin? We made a fire. It was so cold."

The man made sure the door was securely fastened. Then he moved forward into the firelight. The girls noticed that he looked white and drawn and had a bloodstained cloth round his left hand. Anne realised why the stranger had checked on the security of the door. She could hear above the storm the distant howl of a pack of wolves, sounding eerily through the trees. She knew that if they picked up the trail of blood from the man's wounded hand it would lead them unerringly to the cabin.

Trying to keep calm, and hoping that Julie did not realise their danger, she said, "You seem to have hurt yourself. You'd better let us dress your hand for you. We always carry some bandages with us, so sit here by the fire while we see to it."

He began to protest that he was quite all right, but he was obviously exhausted and finally sank down on to the chair.

Julie fetched their first-aid kit from the rucksack, whilst Anne helped him off with his heavy coat. Asked how he came by the wound, he told them that he had tripped over a hidden branch, and his gun, which was loaded, had gone off. The wound could have been made by a bullet, Anne supposed.

Between them they dressed the wound satisfactorily. The stranger gave them a somewhat grudging "thank you". Then, after drinking the contents of a flask of whisky, which he pulled from his coat pocket, he slumped down in the chair and sank into sleep so deep as to suggest unconsciousness brought on by exhaustion and loss of blood.

As Julie threw some more wood on the fire, she became aware that the howling of the wolves was much nearer.

The anxious look on Anne's face indicated that she thought the same thing. The eerie howls drew rapidly nearer.

Anne whispered, "Quick, Julie! Help me pull the bed in front of the door, just in case."

"We're not going to get any help from him," remarked Julie, nodding at the slumbering man.

The bed was fairly heavy. They dragged it across the uneven floor, then stopped, gazing at each other with horrified eyes. The movement of the bed had uncovered a pile of beautiful fur pelts. The same thought was in the minds of both. Were the pelts stolen property?

"He came here to collect them," whispered Anne, and Julie nodded.

They pulled and tugged until the bed was in front of the door, and almost at once the howling rose to a crescendo. The wolf pack circled the log cabin and hurled their heavy bodies furiously against the door. The trail of blood had led them here, and they were hungry!

The noise roused the stranger, who looked towards the door and saw the pelts exposed.

Stumbling to his feet he shouted angrily, "So you have spy on me? So! I will——!"

He could not finish. Reeling dizzily, he fell forward on to the bed, overcome with pain and weakness.

Julie adjusted the sling on his arm, and Anne covered him with the few ragged blankets that served for bedclothes.

Hurriedly now, Julie replenished the fire. Anne picked up the gun, which the man had left near the door, and stood looking anxiously through the frost-

Reeling dizzily, he fell forward on to the bed

covered pane that served as a window.

The storm abated, and a weird light illuminated the prowling wolves, who continued to snarl and leap at the walls of the shack, enraged that their prey should be so near and yet out of reach.

Julie tried to keep as calm as Anne, but she shivered in spite of the fire. She was immensely relieved when Anne suddenly announced that the leader of the wolves seemed to have given the signal to depart and search for their supper elsewhere.

"They're gone!" Anne cried.

"Thank goodness!" said Julie fervently.

The wind dropped and only a few flakes of snow continued to fall as the last wolf disappeared into the dark wall of trees beyond the cabin clearing.

The girls sat down thankfully. Anne unloaded the gun, so that the stranger would have no weapon to use when he regained consciousness. She hid the bullets at the bottom of her rucksack. In doing so she found a welcome slab of chocolate, which she shared with Julie.

The man snarled and struck at Duncan

They were both dozing uncomfortably by the fire when they heard a dog barking and sniffing excitedly outside the door.

"It's Breck!" cried Anne. "It's Duncan's dog! My brother must have come searching for us."

Julie rose stiffly, and hurried to help Anne pull the bed away from the door. The man, awakened by Breck's barking, staggered to his feet and made for the gun, which Anne had stood up in the corner of the cabin.

As Duncan flung open the door, he found himself, to his amazement, looking into the barrel of a gun.

"It's all right," said Anne calmly. "It isn't loaded. I took the bullets out."

There were other men behind Duncan. As they ran into the cabin the man with the gun fired. There was a click. The frustrated man let out a snarl, flung the weapon furiously to the ground, and struck out at Duncan.

There was a short, fierce fight, but the wounded man had no chance, and was quickly secured.

Duncan was thankful to find Julie and his sister safe in the cabin. His companions included the trapper Pierre Lachasse, who identified some of the pelts as his. There was no doubt that the man with the gun was a fur-thief. He had been shot in the hand while being chased by a trapper.

They soon set off for home, following Breck as the dog ran swiftly along the trail through the forest and out into the open ground beyond.

Julie's last day had certainly been full of excitement. Julie knew she would often re-live the events of the day, and perhaps hear again the howls of the wolves as she sat by the Guides' camp-fire at home!

A PET FOR PAULINE

"Oh, I wish he was mine!" cried Janice

by Freda M. Hurt

The two Brownies almost pressed their noses against the glass of the pet-shop window in their eagerness to see. They always stopped on the way to and from the Pack meeting to look in the pet-shop.

"Aren't they the darlingest things you ever saw?" cried Janice Janes, with a sigh of rapture.

"Yes," agreed Pauline Huggins. "I like the ginger one best."

"Yes, so do I." Janice jostled Pauline a little, in order to get closer to the cage in which the three kittens played. She waggled a finger against the glass, and the ginger-coloured one pretended it was a butterfly, and patted its side of the window with tiny paws.

"Oh, I wish he was mine! Don't you wish he was yours?" cried Janice.

"Rather," mumbled Pauline, who couldn't say all she felt.

"The two tabbies are perfectly sweet too, but the ginger one——" Even Janice, the chatterbox, could not find words to show how she felt about the ginger kitten.

It was sleek rather than fluffy, with a wee white chin and a white patch on its tummy. Its eyes were still a milky blue, and, in spite of being shut up in a cage, it seemed to be finding life an amusing game. While the Brownies watched, it chased its wisp of a tail, wrestled with its tabby brothers, pounced on imaginary mice, then nosed the glass in front of Pauline and Janice in the friendliest manner.

"Oh, you little love!" exclaimed Janice, and though Pauline only smiled she was staring at the kitten with longing eyes.

Janice, who was Sixer of the Gnomes, was one of a family of three children, and she had an old dog, a white rabbit, and a tame tortoise at home. The dog belonged to the whole family, and the rabbit belonged to her brother Tim, but the tortoise was her very own. In her heart, Pauline envied her. She was an only child, and lived alone with her mother in a small flat. She had no pet at all, not even a white mouse. Her mother said they couldn't keep pets in a small flat with no garden of their own. But how Pauline wished she could have the ginger kitten!

"I could go in for the Animal Lover badge if I had it," she said. "I can't gain the Animal Lover badge without a pet to look after."

A stout, kind-looking woman joined them outside the shop. "The little dears!" she murmured, beaming at the kittens. Then she went into the shop.

"I believe she's going to buy one," whispered Janice, excitedly. "If it's the ginger one I shall ask her if I can stroke it."

Pauline said nothing, but she almost held her breath as the stout woman came to the door with the white-coated shopman and pointed to the kittens.

"Only twenty-five pence, eh?" she said. "Let me see, which one shall I have?"

"Not the ginger kitten, please, not the ginger kitten!" Pauline was saying to her in her own mind. She wanted it for herself so badly. Perhaps if she were to tell her mother just how much she wanted it she would say she could have it.

The stout woman made up her mind suddenly. "Tabby with the white paws," she said. "They say tabbies make good mousers."

"Oh, please don't choose the ginger kitten!" breathed Pauline to herself

Pauline let her breath out again in a sigh of relief. After they had seen the chosen kitten taken from the cage, and had stroked it in the woman's arms outside the shop, the Brownies tore themselves away and went home.

Pauline found her Aunt Muriel at the flat. She was a fussy person, but kind.

"Dear me, it's Christmas the week after next," she said, after she had remarked that "somebody's" shoes made a lot of noise, and "somebody's" hands needed washing. "How it does come round!"

Pauline was looking forward to Christmas, although she knew she would get nothing very exciting in the way of presents. Some of her friends had gifts like bicycles and expensive dolls, but Pauline's mother was a widow, and couldn't afford such things.

"And what would you like me to give you?" asked Aunt Muriel. "Something not *too* expensive," she added hastily.

"Please, I'd like a kitten," Pauline blurted out. "There's a ginger one in the pet-shop along the High Street, and it's only twenty-five pence." She looked eagerly from Aunt Muriel to her mother.

"Now, Pauline!" Mrs. Huggins sounded annoyed. "I've told you again and again that we cannot have a pet while we're living in this tiny flat."

"But, Mummy——" Pauline began to plead.

"No, Pauline." Mrs. Huggins, who was feeling cross and tired after a hard day's work, cut her short. "I don't want to hear anything more about it."

Pauline gulped and was silent. "It's not fair," she told herself, thinking of Janice's home and all the pets there. "It simply isn't fair."

She was grateful to Aunt Muriel, however, when she pressed some coins into her hand before she left. "That's for somebody's Christmas expenses," Aunt Muriel murmured, "in advance—and don't," she added, turning to Mrs. Huggins, "don't make her put it in her money-box."

"All right," smiled Pauline's mother, "though I expect she'll spend it on something quite silly. Children always do."

What should she spend it on? A book? Doll's furniture? A new pen? She had twenty-five pence from Aunt Muriel. The next day she was peering into shop windows with Janice, but she couldn't make up her mind.

"Let's go and see if those kittens are still in the pet-shop," suggested Janice, as they came away from Pack meeting the following Friday.

"All right," agreed Pauline, feeling the

"That's for Christmas," said Aunt Muriel

twenty-five pence in the purse on her uniform belt.

They went round to the pet-shop, and there were the two kittens curled into furry balls, asleep. The ginger one woke up when it heard the Brownies' voices, and looked at them with its head on one side, as if to say, "Hullo! So it's you two again!"

"What a shame your mother won't let you have him!" cried Janice. "After all, you could buy him with your money. You've got twenty-five pence."

Yes, she had enough. Pauline looked longingly at the ginger kitten, who started playing with a straw.

"I say!" cried Janice suddenly, excitedly. "Couldn't you buy him and keep him at *our* place?"

"At your place?" Pauline stared at her blankly.

Pauline came out thrilled with her pet

"Yes. You could come and see him every day there, and perhaps your mother will soon change her mind about letting you have a pet, and then you can take him home."

"But what would *your* mother say?" Pauline frowned, secretly very tempted.

"Well——" Janice hesitated. "She needn't know about it," she said at last. "We could keep him in the shed at the bottom of the garden, where Arthur's hutch is." Arthur was the white rabbit.

"It wouldn't work," said Pauline. "She'd find out."

"She wouldn't," said Janice eagerly. "She hardly ever goes down the garden—not right to the end. And, anyway, she doesn't notice things very much. She's always so busy. I say, Pauline, you could work for your Animal Lover badge then."

Pauline still hesitated. And then a rather unpleasant-looking man stopped and stared in at the kittens. Pauline suddenly thought: "Suppose he buys the ginger kitten and isn't kind to it?" The idea was unbearable. "Come on!" she said to Janice, and ran into the shop. She offered her money and asked for the ginger kitten before she had time to think again.

The shopman put the furry mite into Pauline's eager hands with instructions to take it straight home. Pauline came out of the shop in a kind of dream. Janice was pleased and admiring, and a little fearful now that the deed was actually done. Pauline buttoned the kitten inside her uniform. It pricked her skin as it clung to her vest with sharp little claws and mewed faintly. She stroked its tiny head with two fingers, and felt a thrill to think that she had a pet of her very own at last.

"I shall call him Rusty," she told Janice.

They smuggled Rusty into the shed at

They smuggled Rusty into the shed

the bottom of Janice's garden, without being seen by anybody but Janice's baby sister, who watched wide-eyed from her pram.

"It's a mercy she can't talk yet," giggled Janice. She went to the house and came back stealthily, carrying a doll's cradle for the kitten to sleep in and some milk the baby had left. "You'll have to buy some cat's food, won't you?" she said. "I think I can manage milk for him."

"All right," said Pauline, but she felt a little anxious. It wasn't that she begrudged spending her pocket-money on Rusty. It was just that she wondered if it would go far enough to keep her pet well fed.

While they were making Rusty play with a piece of string, there was a sudden "wuff!" in the doorway, and there stood Boris, the old retriever. Rusty arched its little back and spat bravely at the big dog, and Pauline ran to gather it to safety. But Boris only wagged his tail.

"He won't hurt Rusty. He loves kittens," cried Janice. "The cat next door is his greatest friend, and he always plays with kittens."

Sure enough, when Pauline came eagerly round to see her pet the next day, she found that the sensible little thing had already decided that the dog was harmless, and the two were frolicking together in the shed.

"I've bought a tin of cat's food," said Pauline. "It cost a lot, and I don't suppose it will last more than two days."

"The people next door buy fish-pieces for their cat. They only pay a few pence for quite a lot," said Janice, with a worried little frown. "But how are we going to cook fish?"

"I'll just have to save some of my dinner every day," sighed Pauline, as she watched Rusty gorging.

But she soon forgot the problem of food in her pleasure in the kitten's fun.

Her happiness in her pet only lasted a short time, however, for when she arrived at Janice's two days later she was greeted with a tale of disaster.

"Mummy knows," gulped Janice, her face still showing traces of tears. "It was Boris's fault. He pushed open the shed door and let Rusty out. Mummy was watching, and she went down the garden and found the cradle and saucer and things, so I had to tell her."

"Is Rusty safe?" was Pauline's first question.

"Yes," said Janice, "but Mummy says we can't keep him for you. She—she wants to talk to you."

"You see, Pauline," said Janice's mother, when Pauline had gone slowly in to see her, "it was wrong of you to buy the kitten when you knew your mother didn't want you to have it."

"But—but it's only because we live in a flat," faltered Pauline.

"Well, one day perhaps you'll have a garden like ours, and then you'll be able to keep a cat," said Mrs. Janes, who really meant to be kind. "Now, I think the best thing for you to do is to let me take Rusty back to the shop and ask the man to sell him for you. I'll ask him to be sure he gets a really good home. Don't you think that's best?"

Pauline nodded miserably, seeing no way out. She couldn't trust herself to speak. She told herself that she was a Brownie and mustn't cry. She dared not say goodbye to Rusty, but ran home without another glance at the ginger kitten.

Pauline gasped with surprise at what she saw

She tried not to think of her lost pet during the days that followed, because, when she did, she got a horrid little ache inside her. She even avoided Janice, and was going to pass Mrs. Janes with no more than a mumble when she met her on the way to call for Janice to go to Pack meeting a week later. But Mrs. Janes stopped her.

"Oh, Pauline," she said, with a smile, "somebody has bought your little kitten, and he's going to a home where he will be well looked after. The shopman has returned some of your money, eighteen pence of it. He kept the rest for his trouble. You'll be able to buy something else now—something your mother won't mind you having."

But Pauline didn't feel that she could

A kitten came prancing to meet her

buy anything else, just yet, with the money, and it was still unspent when Christmas Day came.

"A happy Christmas, dear!" said Mrs. Huggins, coming into her bedroom on Christmas morning with a smiling face. "My present is downstairs, so hurry up and dress."

"I wonder what it can be?" thought Pauline. She had one or two ideas about it, but they were nowhere near the truth, for when she entered the dining-room, after a very hurried wash and a scrambled dressing, she gave a gasp of joyous surprise.

A small ginger kitten with a large bow round its neck came prancing sideways across the floor to meet her.

"Rusty!" she cried, scooping the kitten up. "Oh, no, it can't be, it can't be!"

"Yes, it is, Pauline," smiled Mrs. Huggins. "He's my Christmas present to you."

"But, Mummy, you said——" began Pauline, scarcely daring to believe it was true.

"I know, dear." Her mother put an arm round her shoulders and gave her a hug. "I'm afraid I didn't realise how very much you wanted a pet. Mrs. Janes told me all about Rusty and you, and I bought him at once and asked the shopman to keep him for me until Christmas came. He'll just have to get used to living in a flat, I'm afraid. I spoke to the people downstairs about him, and they seemed to like the idea of a cat about the place."

With a sigh of pure happiness, Pauline put her cheek against the soft, furry little body. "I should think *anybody* would like my Rusty," she said.

And the ginger kitten purred loudly.

THE EDITOR CHATS

Some people will think that I ought to have put my chat with you at the beginning of the *Brownie Annual*, instead of at the end, but I thought you would rather read exciting stories and other contributions before hearing what I'd got to say. All I hope is that you won't find *this* page dull after what has gone before!

Since the last *Brownie Annual* came out, I have moved to a new house in a country lane, and I think I have learned enough to qualify for the Discoverer badge! You can learn lots about Nature and the out-of-doors from books, but living in the country you pick up all kinds of interesting, out-of-the-way titbits of knowledge that you never find in books.

My house is bordered by meadows. I was mowing the lawn the other day and happened to look up. Staring at me over the hedge was a great big face! Do you know whose the face was? It belonged to a cow, who'd heard me mowing and had hurried over the

meadow for the grass cuttings! The rest of the herd ambled up, too, and gave loud "moos" to tell me they were waiting for a feed of nice, tasty minced grass!

Keep the Countryside Tidy

When you go into the country be very careful not to drop sweet or chocolate wrappings, or leave litter about after a picnic, won't you? Not everybody is careful about keeping the countryside tidy. When the Scouts and Cub Scouts held their Scout Job Week, I gave three Cub Scouts the

job of collecting cigarette packets, scraps of paper and other unsightly bits and pieces from our country lane. Two Brownie sisters helped. Do you know how much they collected? Two dustbins full! Just imagine what our lovely country lanes, hills, meadows and grass-verges would look like if everybody was as careless and thoughtless as the people who over a period had scattered two dustbinfuls of odds and ends along one pretty country lane!

Rook Raiders

We get many kinds of birds in our garden, and very fascinating they are to watch. I saw something in early spring that quite astonished me. Rooks were busy building their nests in the tall elms opposite our house. Do you know where some of their material came from? From the backs of the cows grazing in the meadows! Those impudent rooks swooped down and pulled out pieces of fur with their beaks from the backs of the cows! I have never heard of birds doing that before—have you?

Tits are just as enterprising. Every morning they help themselves to the cream from the tops of the milk bottles at the door by pecking through the foil. During nest-building time they flew on to some blankets hung out to dry in our back garden after being washed and pulled the fluff out to use as a soft lining for their nests! The impudence of it!

One morning I saw a small reddy-brown shape moving swiftly along

Nature study with Tawny

the hedge dividing our garden from the meadow. Guess what it was! It was a weasel. He'd come for some of the scraps that had fallen from the bird-table. The weasel is smaller than the stoat, but otherwise I don't think there is much difference between the two. Both have very sharp teeth and are brave and fierce fighters. The weasel I saw would have done credit to any Brownie Pack in one way. He was perfectly groomed! His coat was sleek, spotless and shining. I shouldn't be surprised if he doesn't say to his little family of weasel children back home among the roots of a tree: "Now, always remember, Willie, Wally and Winifred, even if you're only going out hunting for food, wash yourself thoroughly, comb your hair, brush your whiskers, and smooth down your skin. You never know whom you might meet. Your mother will agree. And you, Winifred, remember, a shiny nose may not look nice on a human girl, but there's nothing so attractive in the weasel world as a good, moist, healthy, shiny nose!"

I thought as I watched the weasel hurry back with a piece of meat in his mouth that as I had a weasel family as near neighbours I certainly shouldn't be troubled with rats or mice.

The Golfing Cat

Talking about rodents reminds me of a curious story I heard about a cat. Golfers playing on a golf-course kept losing their balls, which disappeared from the green on which they landed. As the loss of a ball ruins the round, as well as being expensive, the golfers naturally took steps to find out where the balls went to. Guess who'd had

"Three ducks on a pond; a green bank beyond"

going in for a three-legged race. I found it was quite easy to come a cropper when your leg is tied to somebody else's!

Pack Ventures by Night

I have been most interested in hearing about the Ventures that

them! The thief was a cat who lived in a house near the golf-course. If this pussy had been a Brownie she'd easily have gained her Collector badge—but not quite in the right way! She'd bagged no fewer than sixty balls. She'd made quite a distinct path through the undergrowth through which she'd padded to the green from her house to fetch the balls, which she'd carried away in her mouth!

Brownie Sports and Revels

During the summer I attended several Brownie revels and sports and enjoyed them as much as the Brownies did—and that's saying a lot! Not only did I compete in a wheelbarrow race for parents, with a Brownie as the wheelbarrow (and came in last but one), but I was roped in—and I mean *roped*—to provide practice, one after the other, for Brownies who were

Photo: Robert Moss

Two on a space-hopper – and one nearly off!

HELPING AT HOME: Helen Cradock, of the 1st Aston Pack, Oxon, is on the Brownie Footpath and is lending Mum a hand by shopping, laying the table and putting away the cutlery after wiping up

Brownie Guide Packs have thought up and carried out during the year. Some have been quite original. As I thought you would all like to know about Ventures other Packs have done, I have had actual Pack Ventures illustrated on the endpapers of this *Brownie Annual*, pages 2 and 3 and 126 and 127, with a brief note underneath each telling what the Venture was. I hope these will start you thinking of new Ventures, perhaps novel and unusual as well as helpful ones. Did you know that you can now go on a Pack Venture that will keep you away from home for a night? That sounds exciting, doesn't it? You have to get the District Commissioner's permission for it—and your parents', of course!

Perhaps if you mention this to your Guider in Pow-wow she might invite suggestions for an overnight Pack Venture.

I do hope you'll enjoy every single page in the *Brownie Annual*, your very own annual, which this year has taken on an exciting "new look".

Best wishes to you all,

THE EDITOR

Brownies climb a rope–ladder at Guide camp

Photos by W.J. Beer

A new Brownie of the 31st Portsmouth Pack makes her Promise

PACK VENTURES

Here are a few more Pack Ventures carried out by Brownies in various parts of the country

221st ROWNTREE, WARWICKSHIRE
1. Knitted toys and sent them to Biafra

266th LIVERPOOL, LANCASHIRE
2. Made up and acted a play, then held a sale and gave proceeds to parents who had lost children in a fire

1st CULTS, ABERDEEN
3. Made felt cats and carol books, which they gave to children in hospital

1st CHIDDINGFOLD, SURREY
4. Baked small cakes for a penny each and raised 14/- for "Shelter"

11th SMETHWICK (WEST SMETHWICK METHODIST), WARWICKSHIRE
5. Carried out a sponsored walk of two hours for the church building fund